A SHORT INTRODUCTION TO
COUNSELLING
PSYCHOLOGY

Short Introductions to the Therapy Professions
Series Editor: Colin Feltham

Books in this series examine the different professions which provide help for people experiencing emotional or psychological problems. Written by leading practitioners and trainers in each field, the books are a source of up-to-date information about

- the nature of the work
- training, continuing professional development and career pathways
- the structure and development of the profession
- client populations and consumer views
- research and debates surrounding the profession.

Short Introductions to the Therapy Professions are ideal for anyone thinking about a career in one of the therapy professions or in the early stages of training. The books will also be of interest to mental health professionals needing to understand allied professions and also to patients, clients and relatives of service users.

Books in the series:

A Short Introduction to Clinical Psychology
Katherine Cheshire and David Pilgrim

A Short Introduction to Psychoanalysis
Jane Milton, Caroline Polmear and Julia Fabricius

A Short Introduction to Psychiatry
Linda Gask

A Short Introduction to Psychotherapy
edited by Christine Lister-Ford

A SHORT INTRODUCTION TO
COUNSELLING
PSYCHOLOGY

Vanja Orlans with Susan Van Scoyoc

Los Angeles • London • New Delhi • Singapore • Washington DC

First published 2009

SAGE Publications Ltd
1 Oliver's Yard
55 City Road
London EC1Y 1SP

SAGE Publications Inc.
2455 Teller Road
Thousand Oaks, California 91320

SAGE Publications India Pvt Ltd
B 1/I 1 Mohan Cooperative Industrial Area
Mathura Road
New Delhi 110 044

SAGE Publications Asia-Pacific Pte Ltd
33 Pekin Street #02-01
Far East Square
Singapore 048763

Library of Congress Control Number: 2008929526

British Library Cataloguing in Publication data

A catalogue record for this book is available from
the British Library

ISBN 978-1-4129-4641-4
ISBN 978-1-4129-4642-1 (pbk)

Typeset by C&M Digitals (P) Ltd, Chennai, India
Printed in Great Britain by The Cromwell Press Ltd, Trowbridge, Wiltshire
Printed on paper from sustainable resources

CONTENTS

ABOUT THE AUTHORS

Vanja Orlans, PhD, Dip. GPTI, AFBPsS, is a chartered coun-selling psychologist, a chartered occupational psychologist, a UKCP Registered Psychotherapist, a Foundation Member with Senior Practitioner Status, BPS Register of Psychologists Specialising in Psychotherapy, and Visiting Professor at Middlesex University. She has extensive training and experience in a range of approaches to therapeutic work, as well as in the understanding of group and orga-nizational dynamics, and has been working with individuals and groups in many different settings for over 20 years. Vanja is currently Joint Head of the Integrative Department at the Metanoia Institute in London, and Programme Leader of the BPS accredited Doctorate in Counselling Psychology and Psychotherapy by Professional Studies (DCPsych), a joint programme with Middlesex University. She also runs a private practice in psychotherapy, counselling, coaching and supervision.

Susan Van Scoyoc, BSc, MSc, is a chartered counselling psychol-ogist, a chartered health psychologist, and a Foundation Member with Senior Practitioner Status, BPS Register of Psychologists Specialising in Psychotherapy. She is currently Registrar for the Qualification in Counselling Psychology at the British Psychological Society and Past Chair of the BPS Division of Counselling Psychology. Susan is also an Integrative Psychotherapist with a spe-cial interest in relationships, and a registered 'expert witness' work-ing in areas such as human rights, family law and cognitive testing.

PREFACE

What is counselling psychology? This is a frequent question, both from those who are seeking to understand the work of counselling psychologists and at times from counselling psychologists themselves. In the course of undertaking and working on this project we have had many long conversations in which we sometimes could answer this question and at other times became confused or unconfident. This left us curious about the links between our experience and the field itself. A number of themes emerged for us as a result of this reflective process and the research which we have undertaken for this book.

Firstly, there is the fact that counselling psychology appears to sit somewhere between scientific psychology, at least as traditionally defined, and the more creative realm of artistry, reflection and self-awareness. A series of polarities and related tensions appeared to inhabit the field – male/female, hard science/soft science, thinking/feeling, subjective/objective, doing/being, one theory/many theories.

Secondly, it appeared that a perspective on these tensions which could constitute a clear identity had yet to be defined, made more difficult in our view by the gradual separation of mainstream psychology from its parent discipline of philosophy. We came to recognize what a challenge it is to articulate a coherent professional identity; the field is so wide ranging, encompassing potentially so many approaches. It seemed to us that the identity of this profession would be better encapsulated by the capacity to *hold* tensions rather than to resolve them.

Thirdly, it seemed to us that our personal experiences of these issues could reflect both individual and institutional dynamics in that a number of issues could manifest at either level. We considered that it might be the challenging nature of these tensions and dynamics, and the resulting difficulty of articulating a conclusive or collective position, that contributes at times to the dilemma of making a clear choice and taking a stand, and to an apparent lack of clear 'speaking out' in favour of the field, at least in the wider professional community.

In researching areas for the different chapters we came to see how wide-ranging and complex the field of counselling psychology actually is. The profession sits somewhat uncomfortably in the family of psychologies – indeed, if we accept that metaphor we could view the system as a whole as a somewhat dysfunctional family. Counselling psychology itself is dogged by philosophical complexities, an enormously wide theoretical span, and a vast array of practice locations. However, we might also view counselling psychology as the 'carrier' of challenges and difficulties that should actually be shared with other members of the 'family'. At the start of this project we felt somewhat daunted at the idea of attempting to find a way through these complexities. Having negotiated these challenges (for now) we have come up with what we think are some interesting ideas about these complexities, and have done our best to speak out in favour of a professional field to which we are both committed. In a sense we have attempted to rise to the challenge posed by Sequeira (2005) in reporting the comment from a meeting of the Division of Counselling Psychology in the British Psychological Society that as a profession 'we are very good at listening but we have to start speaking!' (p.1). In this book we have set out the issues as we currently see them, where possible putting forward facts, and where we are dealing with opinion to make this clear to the reader. Some of our ideas may be contentious among our colleagues and in those cases we welcome more discussion and debate as the field of counselling psychology matures even further. At the heart of counselling psychology lies the recognition, and indeed the celebration, of the subjective and the intersubjective and our aim in writing this book was to mirror this process in the book itself.

In the following pages we tackle the issue of what counselling psychology is and might be. Each chapter is relatively self-contained, so we invite the reader to review the chapter descriptions in the contents and start wherever their interest takes them, returning to other sections at a later date. While we include much information of particular relevance to the professional situation in the UK, we also address a number of issues pertaining to counselling psychology in a range of countries around the globe. We have a strong interest in collaborating more consistently with colleagues from different countries, and in sharing challenges and difficulties as well as a vision for the field of counselling psychology. To this end we particularly welcome any comments or issues evoked by our ideas among colleagues in other countries. In Chapter 1, we set out the social and historical context of the field as a whole, both within the UK and internationally, consider some of the institutional factors and dynamics that surround the profession, and outline the values that are embedded in the practice of this work. Chapter 2 tackles the issue of the philosophical basis to counselling psychology, a matter which is currently a live and often contentious one in professional settings, especially in the context of accredited training programmes in counselling psychology. We review the historical separation of the parent discipline of philosophy from the discipline of mainstream psychology, consider a number of developments which have run counter to this trend, and review what we might broadly think of as current postmodern perspectives which have a relevance to the field. We conclude this chapter with a consideration of the location of counselling psychology within the tensions and debates highlighted.

Chapter 3 develops these ideas further and outlines the professional knowledge base that underpins the practice of counselling psychology in its many different forms. This chapter includes a review of the major traditions in the psychological therapies that practitioners draw on in this field, together with related research. We also highlight the role of reflexivity as a key characteristic of the profession, and consider the implications of this emphasis more generally for research and practice. Chapter 4 provides a review of professional training in the field of counselling psychology, with the predominant focus on the UK, but with a consideration also of global perspectives. We outline information on training structures, routes to qualification, university and non-university locations for training, as well as recent developments in curriculum philosophy and design. We highlight the current demands that face trainees, especially in the UK where training programmes are now required to offer doctoral level study, a change which carries a number of potential implications for the development of the field. In this context also we discuss the role of personal therapy and the related debates that this has thrown up over recent years. Finally, we highlight some of the challenges that trainees face, as well as requirements for on-going supervision and continuing professional development.

Chapter 5 addresses the issue of what qualified counselling psychologists actually do and outlines the many different settings in which the profession plays a key role, highlighting also the actual tasks and activities which are a part of each role and its related context. Our aim is to demonstrate the very wide range of work settings that are potentially available and relevant to qualified professionals, depending on their own interests and specific forms of training and development. In this chapter also, we include a number of vignettes from individuals actually working in the settings outlined. Our final chapter considers a number of key debates and challenges that are currently very alive in this professional field. We review the position of counselling psychology within the wider field of the psychological therapies and address a number of political considerations which are currently facing the profession, notably the move towards statutory registration. We also consider the question of boundaries between the different helping professions, and some recent perspectives on training considerations. We conclude with some of our own personal reflections on this field. In the appendices the reader will find information on a range of resources relevant to the profession which will include resources from both the UK and other countries around the world.

The details included in the book are designed to be a resource for anyone who is thinking about training and working as a counselling psychologist – not just the bare facts – however, those can probably be gleaned from relevant websites. We also consider the implications of different facts, offering potential trainees an opportunity to reflect more deeply on what they might be undertaking in making a commitment to this field. Our reflections on current tensions and possible ways forward in the profession will, we hope, be of interest also to qualified practitioners and more senior colleagues, and importantly, to colleagues in other countries across the world. We have both worked in this field for a long time and have enjoyed the opportunity of setting out a number of key debates in this profession so that they can be taken further by the reader. As this book also takes its place as one in a series of volumes on different therapeutic professions, we hope that the distinctive nature of counselling psychology comes through.

Vanja Orlans
Susan Van Scoyoc
August 2008

ACKNOWLEDGEMENTS

A special thank you to our colleagues, Paul Hitchings and Patricia Moran, who provided comments and feedback on the developing manuscript. Our warm gratitude also to clients, supervisees, students and BPS colleagues who have contributed so much to our learning, to all at Sage who have been endlessly patient and supportive, and to our families and friends who have lovingly put up with our physical and psychological absence as we worked on this project.

1
THE SOCIAL AND HISTORICAL CONTEXT OF COUNSELLING PSYCHOLOGY

Our aim in this opening chapter is to set the scene for the reader, to locate the profession of counselling psychology within its wider historical, social and occupational context both within the UK and internationally, and to facilitate an understanding of the framework in which counselling psychology operates. We shall also include a review of the value base of a profession which is now established in the UK, its preoccupation historically with well-being as opposed to illness, with context, and with the inclusion in its practice of a range of theoretical perspectives. When we state that the profession is now an established one, we are talking about a span of 25 years since the first formal structures of the profession were put in place in the UK. When compared, for example, with counselling psychology in the USA which began in 1946, the profession of counselling psychology in the UK is still relatively new. It may therefore be helpful for the reader if we provide a brief summary of how this profession came into being.

Professional developments in the UK and Ireland

A new initiative in the British Psychological Society (BPS) traditionally starts with the formal establishment of an interest group. This provides a forum where people with similar interests and excitements can meet and discuss their work and their ideas. During the 1970s there was an increasing number of individuals who had gained a first degree in psychology and who had gone on to do counselling training, or 'helping' work of some kind, and who had no place within the BPS where they felt they could 'settle' professionally. Both of us were among those graduates, each of us exploring a number of possibilities for professional advancement. Colleagues meanwhile were lobbying the BPS on our behalf, culminating in what Nelson-Jones (1999) points to as the conception of counselling psychology in September 1979, when the Professional Affairs Board of the BPS set up a working party to consider the relationship between psychology and counselling (BPS, 1980).

Nelson-Jones (1999) highlights a number of contextual factors which are likely to have influenced the timing of the BPS Working Party's emergence. The counselling movement in the UK was well underway, emphasizing help for the 'worried well' rather than those who were 'mentally ill'. Voluntary agencies providing such services were being established. The Marriage Guidance Council (now Relate) had already been established in 1938; the first university counselling service had been offered at Keele in 1963, with the Association of Student Counsellors having been formed in 1970. There had been a significant development of careers counselling over that time in the UK, with this service being offered both in schools and in work settings. One of us (Vanja) did an MSc in Occupational Psychology in the late 1970s where careers counselling, plus the links between the professional and the personal as seen through a counselling framework, formed key components of the core curriculum on that programme. In the wider international setting, there was also the influence of the post-1960s organizational development activities, often based on reflective and humanistic principles as well as helping models (e.g., Argyris, 1970). In 1977, the British Association for Counselling (BAC, now BACP) was established, a significant event which created a professional framework for counselling and signalled the advent of organized training.

The main aim of the BPS Working Party was to assess the extent to which counselling was a legitimate activity for a psychologist and the extent to which such activity could professionally be located and supported within the remit of the Society. The Working Party directed its attention to a very wide range of sources of information, focusing, for example, on definitions of counselling and ways in which this activity could be distinguished from psychotherapy; on training programmes for counsellors and related standards; on professional and ethical guidelines for such work; on the relationship between counselling in the UK and other countries; and on the potential relevance to counselling of psychological research. The role played by counselling within psychology departments was also explored, as was the international setting, and the existence of the profession of counselling psychology in the USA, Canada and Australia. In its final report, the Working Party supported the recognition of counselling as an activity based in the understanding of psychological processes. While there were a number of options open for recommendation, the Working Party settled on the option that the Society establish an interest-based Section of Counselling Psychology. The establishment of this Section in December 1982 is generally regarded as the birth of the profession of counselling psychology within the UK. At the end of that first year the Section had 225 members.

Continuing progress was supported by the launching of the *Counselling Psychology Section Newsletter*, which in 1986 became the *Counselling Psychology Section Review*, and in 1989 the *Counselling Psychology Review* (Woolfe, 1996). It was to take some time, however, before counselling psychology took its full professional place as a Division of the BPS. David Lane (Lane and Corrie, 2006a), who was a member of the Committee of the Counselling Psychology Section at that time, describes how they sought divisional status but were rejected on the grounds that the professional area was not at that time regarded as sufficiently defined to warrant this; instead the BPS suggested a compromise position whereby a 'Special Group' in counselling psychology be established. The Special Group developed its own practice guidelines and was to function as a kind of 'half-way house' between a scientific interest group and a professional body (Strawbridge and Woolfe, 2003). While this development was widely viewed as a stepping stone to later divisional status, there was still much to be negotiated in order to attain that later status. David Lane refers to 'fierce resistance' both from other divisions within the society and from within the ranks of the Special Group. We reflect later on the nature of this resistance, and some of the underlying factors that may have contributed to it.

Notwithstanding the resistance, the field continued to evolve with an important development represented by the establishment of the BPS Diploma in Counselling Psychology. This offered a training framework and a curriculum that defined an area of theory and practice for the profession. Finally, in 1994, divisional status was achieved, allowing graduates of the Diploma in Counselling Psychology, or others who gained the Statement of Equivalence to the Diploma, to call themselves Chartered Counselling Psychologists. Until the formation of the Division of Counselling Psychology there had been no formally recognized route to Chartered Status for those with a psychology degree and subsequent training in counselling or psychotherapy. Both of us had been in that position, Susan with training in Family Therapy, and Vanja with training in Gestalt Psychotherapy, the Person Centred Approach and group work. By the end of the year in which the Division was established, it had become the second largest division of the BPS after Clinical Psychology, with 1164 members. At the time of writing, the Division of Counselling Psychology has 1947 members, making it the third largest division in the BPS after clinical and occupational psychology. Recent developments have included an emphasis on geographical spread across the UK and the establishment of national branches of the Division of Counselling Psychology in Scotland and Wales. Training in counselling psychology has also continued to grow over the years, with the current provision both of an independent route and course routes to chartered status.

In 2004, a special edition of the professional journal *Counselling Psychology Quarterly* was devoted to 'counselling psychology across the western world', and while counselling psychology in the UK was referred to, there was no mention of Ireland or the development of counselling psychology within the Psychological Society of Ireland (PSI). Apart from the close historical and geographical links between Britain and Ireland, the two countries have had close professional links at university level, as well as in a mutual consideration of standards in the field of counselling psychology. An outline of the development of counselling psychology in Ireland is provided by Hannan (2001, cited in Cunningham, 2004) who highlights the establishment of the profession in that country since 1997. In 1989, a Counselling and Therapy Interest Group was established in PSI; in 1995 this was renamed the Counselling Psychology Interest Group and had more than 80 members. Division status was achieved in 1997 and by 1999 there were 96 members. Since that time membership has more than doubled, and currently stands at 210. The first professional training course to masters level, which began as a one-year diploma, was established at Trinity College, Dublin (TCD) in 1988, with masters programmes in University College Cork (UCC) and University College Dublin (UCD) beginning in the same year. Accreditation criteria for training in counselling psychology were established by PSI in 1993, with the TCD and UCD courses achieving accreditation. A particular challenge for counselling psychology in Ireland arises from the political situation with regard to Northern Ireland – part of the same land mass with an associated identity, but historically also a part of the UK. This situation has created some professional recognition problems for qualified practitioners in that area, with a leaning towards acceptance only of BPS qualifications within statutory services in Northern Ireland.

International perspectives

While the profession of counselling psychology exists formally in a number of countries, there are other countries in which this is not yet the case but where professional activities traditionally associated with the practices of counselling psychology can be identified. Information derived from all of these settings throw light on the professional development of counselling psychology as a specialty in its own right, as well as highlighting some of the challenges currently facing the profession, both in the UK and elsewhere. Our research has resulted in the conclusion that we are in the company of a wide international pool of varied and interesting colleagues, all pursuing worthwhile projects and making a stand for things that matter, often in the name of counselling psychology, but more importantly perhaps, based on values that underpin the development and practice of this profession. In our account below, we include these findings and reflect later on the commonalities between our different concerns and on ways that we might support each other more coherently.

Counselling psychology, as a formally recognized profession, exists, at the time of writing, in the UK, Ireland, the USA, Canada, Australia, New Zealand, Hong Kong, Korea and South Africa, although counselling psychology as a potential professional grouping of practitioners exists also in other countries. A number of contextual and social factors appear to be relevant here, both in terms of where counselling psychology has a clear professional identity and where it does not. Apart from the statutory recognition achieved in these countries, counselling psychology has now been given division status in the International Association of Applied Psychology (IAAP). This came about at the 2002 Congress of Applied Psychology in Singapore, where the Board of Directors of IAAP voted to create Division 16, The Division of Counseling Psychology (Leong and Savickas, 2007). As part of this development, a special issue of the journal *Applied Psychology: An International Review* was planned, to consider the discipline of counselling psychology in 12 different countries across the world. Authors were selected from the membership of IAAP and were asked to conduct their own SWOT analyses (Strengths, Weaknesses, Opportunities, Threats) on the current state of the profession in their country and their vision for the future. Individuals invited to take part in this analysis were senior people in the field within their own countries. Authors who wrote the different articles came from the USA, Australia, Canada, Japan, Korea, India, China, Hong Kong, Israel, Portugal, France and South Africa, places with either an established or developing identity in the field. We have also had access to relevant information on the professional situation in Germany and Greece. In the following sections we provide more detail on professional issues relevant to the field of counselling psychology in each of the countries referred to above, together with any assessments about future possibilities. Finally, we consider some of the commonalities and differences that may be identified on the basis of this information.

Counselling psychology in the USA and Canada

The USA has the longest established independent profession in counselling psychology. In 1946 the American Psychological Association (APA) reorganized itself into divisions with Division 17, Personnel and Guidance Psychologists, formed to meet the professional demands already identified in those areas (Doll, 1946). Much of the work at that time was focused on providing career or educational guidance to combat veterans – in fact, the USA Veterans Administration (VA) is regarded as a key influence on both the emergence and later professional development of counselling psychology in the USA (Whiteley, 1984; Munley et al., 2004). Within a few years this division was renamed Division 17, Counseling and Guidance, a change which reportedly came about through senior members of Division 17 using the term 'counseling' rather than 'personnel'. It is likely that this language change was also influenced by the growing popularity of counselling within the USA at that time. This was in large part driven by the awareness raised by Carl Rogers (also a psychologist) who in 1942 had published his first book, *Counseling and Psychotherapy*, followed in 1951 by his major work *Client Centered Therapy*. Following an important conference sponsored by Division 17 in 1951 on the training of counselling psychologists, the impetus was set in motion for a further name change to Division 17, Counseling Psychology, and the confirmation of this field as a specialty (APA, 1956).

In 1974, the foundation of the National Register of Health Service Providers in Psychology provided a focus for discussions about the training and accreditation of counselling psychologists in the USA, with developments which included the specification of 'psychology' in the title of accredited programmes, and the development of doctoral level training for counselling psychologists (Gelso and Fretz, 2001). Among the training needs identified for counselling psychologists was a particular emphasis on diversity and a greater understanding of cultural identities. These developments were in line with the humanistic value base of counselling psychology, as well as responses to the changing social world in the USA following the civil rights movement, the Vietnam War, the demands of underrepresented social groups, and the rise of feminism. As a result of these concerns, Division 17 was reorganized during the early 1990s to allow for more emphasis on diversity within its structure. In 2003, the Division changed its name to the Society of Counseling Psychology, promoting an explicit emphasis on 'unity through diversity' (Munley et al., 2004). The Society of Counseling Psychology has proved to be popular as a division within the APA, and currently has the second largest division membership after clinical psychology. Training programmes to date remain generalist, designed to serve a wide range of settings and presenting issues (Leong and Leach, 2007). The majority of training programmes are located in psychology departments, with a minority located within departments of education. Leong and Leach (2007) report an increased blurring of the boundaries between clinical and counselling psychologists, with both professional groups working in similar environments.

The profession of counselling psychology in Canada evolved originally from a diverse set of interests spanning the fields of both psychology and counselling (Lalande, 2004). Two national organizations are recognized as having influenced the development of this field, the Canadian Psychological Association (CPA) and the Canadian Counselling Association (CCA). In 1986, counselling psychology in Canada gained recognition as a specialty in its own right with the establishment of the Section of Counselling Psychology within the CPA. The Section identifies a framework for the practice of counselling psychology together with an emphasis on specialist training for this field. The term 'psychologist' is a licensed one in Canada, with all regions having regulatory frameworks in place; however, the specifics of what needs to be done to attain a licence appears to vary across different regions. The CPA outlines the requirements for training in the different regions, with requirements covering both doctoral and masters level. Although practice requirements are set out for different regions there is much variability, and in some areas certain settings are exempt from some of the requirements (Lalande, 2004). The influence of the wider field on the profession of counselling psychology in Canada appears to be in evidence on the CPA Section of Counselling Psychology's website where we see frequent reference to 'counselling' as the profession, rather than 'counselling psychology'. Young and Nicol (2007) highlight external influences and competition from other groups as a threat to the profession, making it more difficult to articulate an agreed definition of the field, or to co-ordinate training standards. Dobson (2002) on the other hand, has emphasized the lack of funding for applied psychology in general in Canada, limiting both the availability and expansion of psychological services. One interesting aspect of counselling psychology in Canada arises from the fact that officially the country is bilingual and multicultural, yet the development of counselling psychology appears to have taken somewhat different routes in the French-speaking and English-speaking areas. Training programmes in counselling psychology are not offered at any of the four major French language universities in Québec (Young and Nicol, 2007). In the French-speaking parts of Canada there is a greater emphasis on guidance counselling rather than on counselling psychology, and there may be some links, culturally speaking, with the general situation in France with regard to a reluctance to move towards a counselling psychology profession.

Counselling psychology in Australia and New Zealand

Counselling psychology in Australia has been described as both a relatively young profession and one that is also contained within a small number of university settings. (Brown and Corne, 2004). The early definition of counselling psychology in Australia came about through a need to establish something professionally different from clinical psychology (Williams, 1978), where individuals would not be regarded as mentally ill, and where the emphasis was more directly on the therapeutic relationship, and less on the techniques that might be employed to bring about change. According to Brown and Corne (2004) the term 'counselling psychology' was first officially used in discussion at the Australian Psychological Society (APS) in 1970. It was some years later, in 1976, that the Division of Counselling Psychologists of the APS was formally established. The establishment of this new profession was also accompanied by an on-going interest in how to advance the profession in the wider field (Penney, 1981). In 1983 the division became the Board of Counselling Psychology, with the current title, the College of Counselling Psychology, being introduced in 1993. While there are many professional counselling organizations within Australia, the College of Counselling Psychology is described as 'the most widespread and the most influential' (Pryor and Bright, 2007, p. 9). Brown and Corne (2004) report a decreasing membership of the College of Counselling Psychology from 904 in 1997 to 774 in 2003, ostensibly as a result of competition with clinical psychology and the fact that economically, clinical psychologists have greater power. However, according to Pryor and Bright (2007) a significant number of psychologists opt to belong to one of the other professional counselling organizations within Australia, taking the emphasis away from jobs in institutional settings (Patton, 2005) and pointing to the growth of private practice. Also, there are only five accredited training courses in counselling psychology throughout the country, all offered by universities. Notwithstanding these factors, counselling psychology as a profession is well recognized in Australia, with work opportunities across a wide range of domains.

Stanley and Manthei (2004) trace the origins of counselling psychology in New Zealand through the initial establishment in 1947 of the New Zealand branch of the BPS, the later establishment of the independent New Zealand Psychological Society (NZPsS) in 1967, the passing of the Psychologists Act in 1981, its subsequent repeal, and its replacement with the Health Practitioners Competence Assurance Act of 2003. During this period there was considerable debate about the management of standards in psychology and a tension between a generic view of applied practice and the articulation of specialties. In 1983, at the annual conference of the NZPsS an interest group of 20 people gathered under the banner of counselling psychology. The first ever counselling psychology symposium took place in the following year, which was followed by a proposal to establish a Division of Counselling Psychology. This Division formally came into being in 1985 with an initial membership of 32. According to Stanley and Mantei (2004) a number of rather quiet years for counselling psychology ensued, with a failure to articulate a separate identity for the field. It was not until 2002 that renewed energy and activity emerged for the Division resulting in 2003 in the establishment of the Institute of Counselling Psychology at the annual conference of the NZPsS. Currently, although still in an *early stage* of development, the field of counselling psychology in New Zealand continues to expand and attract interest and debate, specifically around the potential consolidation of a separate identity and the establishment of a solid training ground.

Counselling psychology in Hong Kong, China, Korea and Japan

This section highlights the varied situations for counselling psychology across these different geographical locations. The Hong Kong Psychological Society (HKPS) now has four professional divisions covering the domains of clinical, educational, industrial/organizational, and the most recent one, the Division of Counselling Psychology which was formally established in 2006 (Leung, Chan and Leahy, 2007).

Professionals who were instrumental in supporting the development of counselling psychology in Hong Kong came from academia, service administration and therapeutic practice, and considered that there should be room for an identity which did not fit the others within the HKPS. The establishment of the new division provides a potential platform for those professionals who identify as counselling psychologists, but who have, to date, been working within the domain of clinical psychology, education, the private sector and the universities (Leung, Chan and Leahy, 2007). Due to the relative lack of formal counselling psychology training opportunities in Hong Kong, this professional group is made up of people who have done a first degree in psychology and then gone on to undertake counselling/therapeutic training. The above authors highlight only one university setting where training in counselling psychology is offered, and in this case within a Faculty of Education with the award being a 'Doctor of Education'. Under these circumstances, individuals who wish to acquire a qualification in counselling psychology are forced to seek this overseas. Notwithstanding these training difficulties, there is still the challenge of gaining a clear identity for counselling psychologists, and distinguishing their practice from social workers, clinical psychologists, educational psychologists and counsellors, particularly as in practice there is much overlap. As Leung, Chan and Leahy (2007) point out, all of these groups engage in assessment activities, case formulation, treatment planning and the process of working through a range of issues with clients. A further challenge is the translation of western theoretical models into a body of clinical literature which has a clearly recognized relevance to the local professional and lay population. There is clearly some way to go in the development of the counselling psychology profession within this setting, but as we later highlight, the challenges posed have some similarity to those faced, for example, by counselling psychologists in the UK.

The situation in China is rather different from that in Hong Kong, notwithstanding the closer association between the two settings since the transfer of sovereignty of Hong Kong to China in 1997. This is largely due to the fact that Hong Kong has always been an international and culturally diverse city, with a significant western influence, and although China has since 1978 opened its doors to a broader influence in the support of economic development, the influence of counselling psychology theories and practices have some way to go. Chang et al. (2005), in a review of counselling and psychotherapy in China, highlight the fact that counselling psychology does not have a clear professional definition in that context, as is the case also for counselling and psychotherapy. In China, these helping professions are all rooted in the medical model and medical settings and as Zhang, Li and Yuan (2001) point out, the practice of psychological therapy, including psychoanalysis, was traditionally carried out in hospitals by medical doctors. As Hou and Zhang (2007) report, the establishment of the Medical Psychology Committee, created in 1979 in the Chinese Psychological Society, was the first committee of its kind in the country. The Chinese Association for Mental Health (CAMH), established in 1985, was also composed mainly of medical practitioners. At the same time, the support of counselling and psychotherapy provided by the medical profession ensured that these psychological practices flourished at least in hospital settings, while consolidating a medical model approach to presenting difficulties.

The rapid rate of change since the political shift from agriculture to industry is seen as positive for the potential of counselling psychology in China (Hou and Zhang, 2007). The open door policy now running for a decade has ensured greater access to western theories and practices as well as an influx of helping professionals from other countries. A particular development highlighted in this context was the extensive series of workshops organized in the late 1980s by the German–Chinese Academy of Psychotherapy (Chang et al., 2005). At the same time, those authors highlight an urgent need for greater psychological resources to meet the current range of psychological problems in the population, a need being given much greater attention by the Chinese government. One factor identified as potentially difficult for the development of counselling psychology in China is the lack of a clear academic and professional relationship between psychology and counselling. More collaboration will be necessary in order to agree on a set of relevant professional codes in the management of mental health problems, as well as agreement on minimal training standards. There is also a substantial challenge in Chinese communities about the acceptance of mental health difficulties and the seeking of relevant help.

In contrast with China, South Korea has a much stronger counselling psychology identity, supported by its recognition as a separate field of study and practice. Originally a part of the Division of Clinical Psychology in the Korean Psychological Association (KPA), counselling psychology achieved its independence in 1987 with the establishment of its own division, entitled the Korean Counseling Psychological Association (KCPA). The division has its own website, publishes the *Korean Journal of Counseling and Psychotherapy* since 1988, and has a large number of members (Seo, Kim and Kim, 2007). KCPA operates a certification system which demands evidence of high standards of training, practice and supervision and which has also been instrumental in promoting the image of a highly trained, ethical and professional group of practitioners. At the same time, training programmes have very different curricula and there is a growing interest in reviewing training requirements so as to achieve greater comparability (Lee, 1996). This highlights potentially the need for a clearer identity, a fact reflected in Seo, Kim and Kim's (2007) identification of the challenge posed to counselling psychologists in Korea by social workers and clinical psychologists in particular, and the increasing number of professional groups that deal with mental health problems.

Watanabe-Muraoka (2007) provides an insightful account of the development of counselling psychology in Japan, and the difficulties of establishing the profession in that country. Although there has been an influx of ideas derived from the American setting, there has been no concerted effort to establish a local professional identity. While there has been some confusion in Japanese society as to the meaning of counselling, some recent clarity has been offered, both by the publication of a key text on counselling psychology (Watanabe-Muraoka, 1996), and by the definition put forward by the Japanese Association of Counseling Science in 2004. At the same time, some confusion continues, with no differentiation made, for example, between clinical psychology and counselling psychology, with the fact that a large number of teachers of counselling are themselves clinical psychologists, and with a tendency within the counselling field to identify with a specific approach or technique rather than a professional orientation. Watanabe-Muraoka's conclusion is that the profession in Japan needs a title that would more clearly speak to current contextual needs; she identifies this as 'lifespan developmental counseling psychology'.

Counselling psychology in South Africa

Counselling psychology has been a recognized and legislated specialty in South Africa since 1974, along with the specialties of clinical, research and industrial psychology (Leach, Akhurst and Basson, 2003). Originally established to report to the Medical and Dental Council, counselling psychology now reports to the Health Professions Council of South Africa (HPCSA), and has its own division within the Psychological Society of South Africa. According to Leach, Akhurst and Basson (2003) six out of the 20 universities in South Africa offer training programmes in counselling psychology, three of these combining theoretical teaching relevant to counselling, clinical and educational settings. Historically, the development of counselling psychology in South Africa is deeply embedded in the apartheid system. The profession first emerged in the context of Afrikaner nationalism, reportedly as a contrast to the more English and liberally identified field of clinical psychology, although the psychology profession as a whole was at that time regarded as racist (Leach, Akhurst and Basson 2003). Currently, counselling psychologists as a professional group comprise approximately one third of all registered psychologists; the majority of the profession as a whole are white, female and work in private practice. Historically, the profession has been heavily criticized for its use, both in training contexts and practice, of theories and models that are not in keeping with the needs of the majority of South Africans (Watson and Fouche, 2007). Research reflects this bias, being skewed in the direction of urban and middle class samples, while the language of the profession does not reflect the languages of the majority population. This has led to counselling psychology being criticized as overly parochial. Watson and Fouche (2007) highlight a number of challenges facing the profession in the context of a transformation in South African society, drawing attention to the need to address a theoretical and research bias, and to foster more collaborative activities which could meet the needs of the society of which it is a part.

Counselling psychology in India

The situation in India is included here as it raises a number of issues relevant to the field of counselling psychology as a whole, which are addressed in a separate section below. Counselling psychology is not an established profession in India, at least in the formal sense. While psychology in India is represented by a number of key professional bodies, including the Indian Association of Clinical Psychologists, there has not been a move to develop a distinct identity for psychologists involved in counselling. A limited number of courses on counselling are on offer, but the quality of training is not monitored for these. What is apparent from a consideration of the situation in India regarding psychology and counselling, is the need for both western and Indian philosophies and ideas to come together to form theories and approaches that have greater face validity to the Indian population and which therefore might more adequately meet identified needs. For example, Arulmani (2007) draws attention to the fact that traditional Indian psychology, referred to as *Mano Vidya*, or 'mind knowledge', is recorded in ancient Indian writings documenting the existence of psychological ideas and techniques that 'bear a startling resemblance to ideas put forth by modern Western psychology and yet predate these efforts by two millennia' (p. 71). Apparently, there is now some activity in this direction, with the development of psychological inventories that draw on traditional Indian psychology (Wolf, 1998). The challenge that these developments present to counselling psychology highlight the need to contextualize concepts and approaches within a framework that can cope with different cultural subjectivities, and by doing so recognize the contextual nature of knowledge and research activity.

Counselling psychology in Israel

According to Benjamin (2007) the lack of recognition of counselling psychology in Israel has not been for want of some concerted efforts by counselling psychologists to gain more visibility and acceptance. A programme in counselling psychology was established in Tel Aviv University in the 1970s, organized by USA trained counselling psychologists, but this programme has recently been abolished, apparently for a range of reasons which include the lack of any holding professional body to accredit graduates of the programme. Psychology in Israel is regulated by the Ministry of Health which has recognized the specialties of clinical, educational, developmental, rehabilitation, medical and social/vocational/organizational psychology. These specialties are also recognized by the Israel Psychological Association (IPA). A proposal to add a division of counselling psychology to the IPA was recently rejected. However, the presence in Israel of a well-established profession in clinical psychology is likely to be a factor in the difficulties of establishing a potentially rival professional group.

While counselling psychology as a specialty in its own right has not flourished in Israel, vocational psychology, as a related field, has been very successful (Robitschek and Woodson, 2006). Activities subsumed under the banner of vocational psychology include career counselling, selection and assessment, and organizational psychology. Given the cultural and social challenges faced by Israel in recent years, these activities have proved to be extremely valuable. Moreover, while not a recognized professional group, counselling psychologists do have a presence, making a meaningful contribution to a range of social and geographical challenges. An example of this, reported by Benjamin (2007) was the recruitment of counselling psychologists to the Israel National Employment Service to help evacuees from the Gaza Strip. This work clearly involved more than a career focus, and took on a holistic quality, with the need to address issues of trauma, grief and crises, as well as the challenges of relocation in terms of vocational demands. The advent of managed care and the growth of new approaches such as coaching have led to an emphasis on skill and competency development within a generic framework. While the Israeli context is very different from that of the UK, there are elements of these developments that mirror some recent thinking within the UK, highlighting the advantages of not over-specifying specialties within applied psychology, but instead promoting a more generic-based and skill-development approach, which can be applied to a range of settings and presenting difficulties.

Counselling psychology in mainland Europe

Counselling psychology does not exist as a recognized specialty in most of mainland Europe, although there are many psychologists who are working within a practice framework which bears comparisons with what counselling psychologists are doing, for example, in the UK. Our research has uncovered a few published papers and some further professional information which give insight into the situation in France, Portugal, Germany and Greece, and we include a summary of the issues in these countries as they currently stand. Even where the specialty is not officially recognized, there are often relevant issues for us to consider in thinking more broadly about the development of the profession of counselling psychology. There are also political factors which come into play, including the mapping of different professions as mutually exclusive. For example, the Strasbourg Declaration on Psychotherapy (European Association of Psychotherapy, 1990) explicitly defines psychotherapy as a separate profession, although the training background of a psychotherapist can take different forms in different European countries, and in some countries will link more directly than in others with psychology training as the initial requirement.

Bernaud, Cohen-Scali and Guichard (2007) present what they describe as a paradoxical situation in France. That is, although counsellors on the one hand work with the theme of 'accompanying' and 'connection', as a professional group there appears to be no interest in forming professional allegiances or identities. These authors point out that the term 'counselling' does not have a direct equivalent in the French language – the nearest work is 'conseil' which translates as 'advice'. Apparently, only one writer in the field uses the actual term 'counseling' in two book titles (Tourette-Turgis, 1996, 1997). While Rogerian ideas on counselling have found their way into French thinking and practice since the 1970s, the practice is generally regarded as very different from 'psychotherapy', the latter seeking to offer psychological assistance of the kind that in the UK we might also ascribe to the majority of counselling practices. They also point out that there is no equivalent in French to the term 'counselling psychology'. It would seem that although the professional title of 'psychologist' is regulated in France, there is no connection directly with the field of counselling as currently defined in that country.

Duarte, Paixão and Lima (2007) provide an overview of counselling psychology in Portugal. Although there are postgraduate programmes available for the training of counselling psychologists, based on a scientist practitioner model and including rather broad based theory as well as skills in the curriculum, there is no professional organization of the field. Also, there appears to be significant competition from other groups of counsellors who have not come from a psychological background. Duarte, Paixão and Lima (2007) refer to career counselling being undertaken by teachers who have no specialist training in that field. These authors define counselling psychology as a specialty that focuses on a person's subjective well-being, and strengthening problem-solving and decision-making skills. The aim would be to 'resolve normative or sporadic crises' (p. 127).

In a research project conducted by the Anglo-German Foundation for the Study of Industrial Society (Lane et al., 2004) the authors report on a study which compared psychology professionals in both countries on a range of work-related dimensions. While there have been attempts by the Association of German Psychologists to create a specialty in counselling psychology these have not been successful. Instead, the professional title in Germany is 'psychological psychotherapist'. Although the title is different, the authors of this report suggest that the two groups are broadly similar. In Germany a four-year degree in psychology to masters level is followed by three-years of full-time training in psychotherapy and one full year of practice. The three main modalities covered are described as psychoanalysis, psychotherapy and behaviour therapy although no detail is given as to what is included in the psychotherapy modality. The results show British counselling psychologists to be relatively optimistic about their profession and the future, whereas their German counterparts were highlighted as very disaffected. The latter finding was put down to the unsatisfactory nature of the legislative framework which now encompasses that professional group, and the feeling that state recognition was undermining for the profession. Sample sizes for the British and German group of psychologists in this study were 317 and 302 respectively.

The Hellenic Psychological Society (HPS) was founded in 1990 in Thessaloniki, with the aim of promoting teaching and research as well as supporting practice across different areas of psychology. HPS has ten divisions including the Division of Counselling Psychology. In Greece the term 'psychologist' and related professional activities are protected by law. A recent development, driven by a Greek colleague of ours, is the establishment of the European Association of Counselling Psychology which was founded in 2006. This association recognizes that most European countries do not have a formally recognized specialty in counselling psychology, but that there are many counselling psychologists in different European countries who have trained abroad and returned with that professional identity. The aim of the association is therefore to support the development and application of counselling psychology in Europe, and is likely to provide a forum for professional exchange as well as networking opportunities. We understand that further developments might include the establishment of a professional journal which could bring together ideas and experiences from colleagues across the European scene. The association already has members from Greece, Malta, Ireland, the UK, Italy and Spain.

Values and tensions in counselling psychology

Our above review of the profession of counselling psychology and its status in many different countries across the globe brings out a number of interesting themes. There is a keenness and protectiveness that comes across about the profession in general, perhaps driven by the fact that it is relatively new in many countries or not even recognized officially in some. There is also the fact that the profession has had to fight relatively hard, over a sustained period of time, for any recognition that exists. A number of factors appear to be relevant in attempting to understand this situation. Firstly, counselling psychology has emerged from a psychological 'field' dominated by positivism and a particular conception of 'science'. Traditional ideas about 'science', especially within western psychology, do not sit easily with the concept of 'the person'. Moreover, the value base of the profession eschews the notion of 'expert', not as a way of denying a skill and knowledge base, but as a fundamental humanistic and democratic position. This raises questions about the interface of counselling psychology with the medical profession which is based on a hierarchy ranging from experts at different levels to patients. Bringing humanistic values into that frame has of course entailed a clash of values in many settings and some considerable effort to find a way through such differences. It would appear to us that these efforts continue in the field at the time of writing, perhaps suggesting that this is itself a characteristic of the profession. Of relevance also, is the competition for finite resources among different professional groups.

Secondly, counselling psychology has been driven by a desire to 'make a stand' – for subjectivity, for the inclusion of context in its research and practice, for promoting well-being as opposed to a focus on illness, for diversity, for the rights of all human beings, and for the right to bring psychology to many different settings. At times, as appeared to be the case in South Africa, these values found themselves sidetracked in the service of political ends. In the UK as we write, there is considerable pressure for counselling psychologists who are working within the National Health Service (NHS) to adopt the 'illness' frame of reference which lies at the core of this service. Such pressure exists in other countries too, and has created tensions and an oppositional frame. It can also foster a desire at times to be even more positivistic than the positivists, a response which is likely to be in part a defence against powerful establishment ideals and values. Many of the issues highlighted here are addressed in more detail in later chapters in the context both of a discussion about the knowledge base of the profession, as well as in the articulation of current dilemmas and debates. For the moment, we hope that we have been able to provide the reader with a 'feel' for the profession, a kind of felt sense of what engaged people to lend their time, energy, and spirit in support of the development of this realm of theory and practice.

What is counselling psychology?

Having reviewed many aspects of the profession of counselling psychology, in many different countries, we would like to end this chapter with a consideration of how we might define this field. This is a challenging task, in part because the profession has both a coherence and, as we have suggested above, can also be defined as the 'different from' position. The official definition, provided by the BPS, is as follows:

> Counselling Psychology is a distinctive profession within psychology with a specialist focus, which links most closely to the allied professions of psychotherapy and counselling. It pays particular attention to the meanings, beliefs, context and processes that are constructed both within and between people and which affect the psychological wellbeing of the person. (BPS website, 2007a)

The emphasis on the importance of humanistic values can be seen in the statements contained in the Professional Practice Guidelines for Counselling Psychology (BPS, 2005a):

> Counselling psychology has developed as a branch of professional psychological practice strongly influenced by human science research as well as the principal psychotherapeutic traditions. Counselling psychology draws upon and seeks to develop phenomenological models of practice and enquiry in addition to that of traditional scientific psychology. It continues to develop models of practice and research which marry the scientific demand for rigorous empirical enquiry with a firm value base grounded in the primacy of the counselling or psychotherapeutic relationship. These models seek:
>
> 1. to engage with subjectivity and intersubjectivity, values and beliefs;
> 2. to know empathically and to respect first person accounts as valid in their own terms; to elucidate, interpret and negotiate between perceptions and world views but not to assume the automatic superiority of any one way of experiencing, feeling, valuing and knowing;
> 3. to be practice led, with a research base grounded in professional practice values as well as professional artistry;
> 4. to recognise social contexts and discrimination and to work always in ways that empower rather than control and also demonstrate the high standards of anti-discriminatory practice appropriate to the pluralistic nature of society today. (pp. 1–2)

We are both in accord with the above guidelines as a succinct and appropriate statement about the profession of counselling psychology, although in our view they do not convey the wide range of attitudes and activities which can be highlighted in different contexts. Also, we recognize that this statement contains a number of philosophical dilemmas and potential conflicts which need constantly to be negotiated. We return to these in more detail in Chapter 2 – for the moment we wish simply to highlight the fact that putting these philosophical ideas and values into practice is not a straightforward matter. It takes courage, is intellectually demanding, and requires a desire to stand for issues that are not always met with a benign attitude (see, for example, Van Scoyoc, 2004). However, in our experience, there is something of the maverick in many counselling psychologists, a quality that is likely either to attract you instantly to the field or send you off looking for something more 'mainstream' and less troublesome.

2

PHILOSOPHICAL CONSIDERATIONS IN COUNSELLING PSYCHOLOGY

We have decided at this point to launch straight into the issue of philosophy and counselling psychology and we very much hope that the experience of considering the ideas set out here will engage you in an energizing way rather than offering you something dry and heavy! This is a very pertinent issue at present in the field of counselling psychology and we think that it raises some important questions and challenges. As we shall see, there are many different philosophical trends that have all influenced this professional field, and there are also many different psychologies, a fact that we shall consider in more detail in the following chapter on professional knowledge in counselling psychology. Our own interest in the philosophical basis to counselling psychology is two-fold.

Firstly, we are personally interested in articulating the deeper story to our clinical work and our teaching and consulting – the identification of elements that lie at the basis of why we are involved in this field and the underlying conceptual framework that is actually driving our decision making and personal energy. Secondly, the issue of philosophy and its identification is currently very alive in professional settings, bringing out tensions, arguments, excitements – a whole range of emotions as well as a number of creative ideas. For example, training courses seeking accreditation are visited by an accrediting team from the Training Committee in Counselling Psychology (TCCP) and one of the boxes that needs to be ticked in the 'Programme Log of Evidence' is entitled 'Core Philosophy'. From our review of the situation across the globe, it would appear that there is a variable interest in this topic – it would seem to us that this issue *as a requirement* is not so pronounced elsewhere, although, as we have seen from the information, for example, on counselling psychology in India, this issue is of crucial importance. We anticipate that colleagues in other countries will be interested in our reflections – as we have seen from the global perspectives in Chapter 1, many of the tensions described have philosophical challenges as their source.

We have been very interested in this process as a whole within the UK – what it is that is difficult in the articulation of a philosophy and where and how professionals locate themselves in these debates. We think that some of these difficulties have to do with the large task that the profession of counselling psychology has taken on in terms of the possible range of philosophical grounds that could be claimed, and the difficulty at times of managing the tension between competing perspectives, values and needs. An extremely poignant element of this process, in our view, is the recognition that over many years of social and intellectual development mainstream psychology became divorced from its parent discipline of philosophy and it seems to have fallen to the field of counselling psychology to consider and manage some form of re-integration. As the original issue and gradual fragmentation was much larger than this particular professional field it is not surprising at times that the task can feel too difficult to manage! In this chapter we set out some of the historical factors involved in the gradual separation of mainstream psychology from philosophy so that the reader can understand the process in more detail. We also identify some counter-developments which are relevant to the field of counselling psychology but which also raise certain challenges. Our goal is to capture a number of significant elements of the unfolding narrative in the development of psychology and to consider specifically the current role of counselling psychology in the light of these developments.

Philosophy and counselling psychology

The word 'philosophy' can be used in a number of different ways, ranging from 'the study of the fundamental nature of knowledge, reality and existence' to 'a theory or attitude which guides one's behaviour' (*Oxford English Dictionary*, 2006). The use of the term 'conceptual basis' in the TCCP guidelines allows for an articulation on quite a wide continuum. The overall interest is in challenging courses and individuals to reflect more deeply on the basis to their work and their training designs, a challenge that we completely support in that it takes us into the reflexive realm and a potentially different form of learning, referred to also as the 'double loop learning' domain (Argyris, 2004) or 'reflection-in-action' (Schön, 1983). In the following chapter, where we address the issue of professional knowledge in counselling psychology, we return to this idea of reflexive practice in more detail. In the context of this chapter, we simply highlight this process as part of the challenge to reflect more deeply on what is actually driving our formulations in our professional worlds.

At the heart of any philosophical investigation, and key to our focus in this chapter, is the exploration of epistemology – that is, that area of philosophy concerned with the nature and sources of knowledge, as well as its limits. At this point, we refer the reader to the statement from the Professional Practice Guidelines for Counselling Psychology (BPS, 2005a) which we set out in Chapter 1. From this statement we can glean that counselling psychology focuses on humanistic ideas of a holistic kind, with the likelihood that the emphasis will be on well-being in the here and now, rather than on ideas of the diagnostic categorization of illness or disorders as derived from a 'medical model' perspective. Practitioners are therefore not likely to see difficulties faced by people in terms of fragmented symptoms to be 'fixed' or cured as quickly as possible. The subjective experience of the person needs to be recognized. Difficulties and distresses are not necessarily regarded as evidence of 'psychopathology' but rather as a potential part of the human condition from birth to death. This raises the issue of the connection of the person with their context and the importance of taking a perspective that recognizes this. However, demands for 'rigorous empirical enquiry' are generally associated with the construction of categories, including the binary notion of 'ill' or 'well', and traditionally separates elements from their context in order to analyze them. The user of psychological tests, for example, focuses on elements not necessarily related to context or the here and now, and has 'cut-off' points and 'scores' with related clinical categorization attached to the outcomes.

From a philosophical point of view, we have quite a conundrum to consider. We have the potential juxtaposition of 'human science research' and 'rigorous empirical enquiry', the idea that there is a measure of philosophical coherence in the 'principal psychotherapeutic traditions', the potential tension between 'phenomenological models of practice' and 'traditional scientific psychology', ideas of 'theory' versus 'practice' as potential sources of professional and possibly philosophical knowledge, as well as questions about practice in relation to research. The name of the profession itself also brings tensions to the foreground, in the bringing together of 'counselling' with 'psychology', and the emphasis potentially on a number of different sets of values which may not necessarily be compatible. Thinking in this way, it becomes clear that counselling psychology sits potentially in a somewhat uncomfortable position within the family of psychologies with its explicit focus on a humanistic value base rather than exclusively on a positivistic scientific belief system. In order to reflect more fully on the potential discomfort of this position, we review below the historical relationship between philosophy and psychology, as well as some significant trends and ideas in the rise of humanism within western philosophical and psychological traditions, the emergence of depth psychology, and the current focus on postmodern ideas. Finally, we consider the position of counselling psychology in the light of these developments. One central issue that we are keen to bring out in this chapter is the challenge of attempting to tackle such a central issue in psychology within one professional field, and perhaps also, the extent to which this is possible.

Historical perspectives on philosophy and psychology

A number of fundamental questions have been addressed by philosophers since time immemorial. Early Greek philosophers (pre-Socrates, Aristotle and Plato) considered three main areas of thought: metaphysics, epistemology and ethics. These considerations lie at the heart of both western philosophical tradition, as well as older non-western traditions. Metaphysics – closely related also to the philosophical domain of ontology that is concerned with 'existence' or 'being' – explores what the world and its components (such as human beings) are made of and seeks understanding of the ultimate substance of reality. Epistemology explores the question of how we come to know what we know, and how we decide what constitutes acceptable knowledge, what is true or false, real or not real. Finally, the study of ethics explores good and bad, right and wrong and is concerned with moral philosophy and morality. Originally, it was philosophy that was the main discipline, and all other disciplines such as physics, mathematics, psychology, and biology, for example, were subsumed within this (Russell, 1961; Leahey, 2004).

The impact of the scientific revolution

A number of factors account for the gradual separation of mainstream psychology from philosophy, at least as separate professional fields. One important set of events was the rise of science in the 17th century. That century saw the invention of the telescope, the microscope, the thermometer, the barometer, the air pump, the discovery of the circulation of blood, advances in pure mathematics and more precise measurements than had ever been possible before. It was a time of complete transformation. Copernicus identified the sun as the centre of the universe, Kepler discovered the laws of planetary motion, Gallileo articulated the laws of dynamics and falling bodies, and Newton discovered that action and reaction were equal. There was the thrilling, and probably anxiety producing, recognition that what had previously been believed might be false; that the test of scientific truth was in the patient collection of facts, combined with the bold guessing about the laws which bound these facts together. All the movements of matter were increasingly identified as being subject to physical laws; it followed that mental events must be equally determinate. As would be expected, philosophical thinking was deeply influenced by these events.

While there were a number of philosophers who made important contributions to ideas at that time, a few stand out in terms of their influence on the emergence of psychology as a separate professional field. According to Leahey (2004), psychology began with the philosopher René Descartes (1596–1650). As Leahey points out, Descartes developed a framework for thinking about the mind and the body and this framework has represented a key focus for psychologists ever since. Descartes is also generally regarded as the founder of modern philosophy, and was one of the most prominent figures in 17th century science. He remains famous for his widely quoted dictum 'I think, therefore I am' which emphasized the separation of mind and matter – according to Descartes, they move alongside each other but cannot act on each other. Descartes' importance lay in the way that he (together with other scientists and philosophers of that time) completely reformulated previous worldviews based on the existence of God in everyday life. What was proposed here was that God had in effect been the creator of a large machine which thereafter was left running. The task for human beings was to figure out the mechanical basis for the running of this machine, a task that we can recognize as on-going in many basic psychology text books. While Descartes did not complete his theory regarding the way in which mind and body interact, partly perhaps because of his own need to fit in with religious ideals of the time, his dualism did emphasize consciousness as a focus for inquiry, and as a mechanism for the control of emotions (Cottingham, 1986). Although there were aspects of these ideas that were not actually new, Descartes' emphasis on what Taylor (1989) has termed his radical reflexivity, paved the way for a later psychological focus on the self and the nature of the thinking process.

Francis Bacon (1561–1626), both a philosopher and a politician, was preoccupied with the possibility of human beings having power over nature, and with the bringing together of rational theory and empirical practice, itself the foundation of technology (Pentonen, 1996). The process of achieving power over nature would be through experiment, with the purpose of utilizing the outcomes as contributions to human welfare. Bacon was instrumental in re-defining key aspects of the role of the scientist and forms of experimentation. Up until that time, the scientific approach emphasized careful observation followed by analysis and the identification of underlying laws. Bacon introduced the idea within science of actively setting up conditions that would then be monitored and evaluated, the key idea in psychology experiments. Thomas Hobbes (1588–1679) was both a scientist and a philosopher, interested particularly in ethics, politics and psychology. In his focus on what he regarded as the central elements of geometry, mechanics and moral philosophy he developed his ideas on civil philosophy and the necessary agreements between individuals in the formation of larger political systems (Peters, 1956). According to Hobbes, the natural laws are inherent in nature and need to be discovered with a view to being incorporated into social systems. He held the view that the senses were instrumental in producing the necessary objective data, and he also linked thinking with language.

John Locke (1632–1704) was interested in the functioning of the human mind, in particular the possibility of radical reflexivity whereby an individual could reflect on his reflections and experiences and employ language to articulate these and imbue them with meaning. His focus on sensation and reflection brings to mind the process of psychological therapy whereby the client externalizes a number of sensations and experiences and then makes sense of these in the context of the therapeutic relationship. He also raised the issue of the freedom of the self and the limits of action. Leibniz (1646–1716) was interested in formal logic and the adoption of a mechanistic view of the world, but he also introduced the idea of conscious perceptions being different from unconscious perceptions and was concerned to understand the relationship between these different states (Broad, 1975). He was interested in the relationship between innate characteristics, consequent development, and overall sense making from pieces of data that might not have been in awareness. We can see in Leibniz the beginnings of that stream of psychology which led later to psychoanalysis. In the interests and activities of these 17th-century philosophers we can discern the gradual separation of a psychological and scientific attitude from the larger philosophical questions, driven particularly by the removal of God from the immediate frame of scientific inquiry.

The rise of industrialism and beyond

The 18th and 19th centuries saw the rise of industrialism, together with political and social changes which brought with them assumptions about people's power over the natural environment, as well as casting the natural environment itself within a scientific frame of reference. Darwin's theory of natural selection raised the issue of purposelessness in the development of the universe, calling into question any transcendent goal. In the context of psychology, it could therefore be posited that moral argument was simply the rationalization of instinctive behaviour patterns (Desmond and Moore, 1991). Darwin (1809–1882) had also been influenced in his thinking by the British psychologist, Francis Galton (1822–1911), who studied variations in human ability and the effects of heredity, and who had a passion for statistics and measurement. As the scientific worldview gained dominance, so did the idea that science could be harnessed to create technology for the achievement of human ends. It was within this context, that Auguste Comte (1798–1857), the French philosopher and social theorist, motivated by the social and moral problems caused by the French Revolution, expressed his three principles of positivism: empirical science was not just a form of knowledge, but was actually the only form of positive knowledge about the world; it was important to move on from the past and do away with mysticism and superstition; an important aim would be to extend scientific knowledge and technical control into human society and into the political and moral domains. By the late 19th century positivism had become a dominant philosophy. The only significant statements about the world were those based on empirical observation.

A further contribution to the development of mainstream psychology's commitment to a positivistic approach came also from the movement known as logical positivism, which originated in Austria and Germany in the early stages of the 20th century. The desire was to develop a system which no longer needed to take account of the controversies that emerged from a metaphysical perspective. The basis of logical positivism is that all knowledge is derived from empirical observation assisted by the use of logic and mathematics. These developments followed the formation of the discussion group known as the Vienna Circle, a group who gathered around Moritz Schlick at the University of Vienna. Both Ludwig Wittgenstein (1889–1951) and Karl Popper (1902–1994) were for a time associated with this group (Frank, 1949). The rise of National Socialism in 1933 marked the end of this movement, although many of its followers emigrated to the USA. Overall, these different events significantly supported the development of mainstream psychology as a separate discipline, distinct in its professional identity from philosophy (Boring, 1957). The view had taken hold that all disagreements about the world could be resolved, in principle, by reference to observable fact. The belief that science would provide the answers to living had arrived.

Given the increasing interest in experimentation in the 19th century it was clear that there would be increasing interest also in bringing issues relating to consciousness and the functioning of the brain into the laboratory, with a view to refining measurements and assessments with a particular focus on quantification. We see here the beginnings of an experimental psychology, later to be made famous institutionally by Wilhelm Wundt. The simultaneous interest in Britain and France in the development of mental testing also supported these trends. In Britain, Sir Francis Galton (1822–1911) worked on the development of tests to measure intelligence, while in France, Alfred Binet (1857–1911), also interested in the measurement of intelligence, focused on more complex levels of assessment and decision making such as those used by expert chess players. These developments formed part of the institutionalization of psychology, and the articulation of the specific rules of scientific experimentation. Danziger (1985) tracks different forms of the development of these rules, identifying different social relationships between researchers and researched in the Leipzig laboratory of Wundt and the Paris laboratory of Binet and his colleagues, and drawing attention to the social nature of knowledge construction.

Wilhelm Wundt (1832–1920), who institutionalized the field of experimental psychology, was Professor of Philosophy in Germany with a doctorate in medicine. He had three major projects: to create an experimental psychology; to create a scientific metaphysics; and to create a social psychology. Although originally founded within a philosophical framework, Wundt's vision implicitly proposed distinguishing philosophy from experimental science, a notion which at the time was quite radical, although clearly pertinent in terms of the previous developments outlined above. Science up to that point had been more commonly based on observations and related calculations. As Leahey (2004) points out, the fields of chemistry and physiology were just emerging during this time, and in medicine it would not be until 1948 that the first clinical drug trial would be officially published. Wundt introduced scientific demonstrations into his philosophy lectures and in 1879 he opened the first psychological laboratory. He also started publishing the first effective 'journal of experimental psychology'. Wundt's interest was in studying 'the contents of consciousness' and in doing this he relied initially on his subjects' introspections. This method was later rejected as unreliable – as it was not directly observable, its validity was called into question. Wundt's activities in effect provided an organizing focus for a number of researchers and theorists and he was instrumental in establishing a lively and collaborative intellectual community within experimental psychology (Danziger, 1990).

Wundt became very famous and had very famous students, including James Cattell (1860–1944) who studied human intelligence and whose goal was to ensure that psychology pursued a scientific path based on the acceptance of quantitative methods. Cattell later became President of the American Psychological Association and although not all of his colleagues agreed with his approach to psychophysical measurement, it nevertheless gained substantial ground, thus allowing experimental psychology to lead the way as a particular specialty within academia. Charles Spearman (1863–1945), whose interest was in general intelligence and who is regarded as the father of classical test theory and pioneer of the statistical technique of factor analysis, was an English psychologist who also worked on his PhD at Wundt's laboratory. Interestingly, George Herbert Mead (1863–1931), well known for his theory of symbolic interactionism, and his belief that the individual is a product of social experience, was also a student at Wundt's laboratory. In general, however, the time was ripe for the development of an experimental approach. The Americans in particular took up experimental psychology with substantial enthusiasm. The first professor of psychology was appointed in Pennsylvania in 1888. Britain was less enthusiastic. A proposal in 1877 to set up a psychology laboratory at Cambridge had been rejected indignantly by the Senate on the grounds that it would be tantamount to putting the human soul in a pair of scales (Farr, 1983). It was not until almost 1900 that laboratories were opened at Cambridge and London University.

The dominant trend throughout this period was one of an increasing fragmentation of elements of psychological exploration which included topics such as sensation, memory and perception. It was assumed that together these elements could potentially form a whole which as a field would be labeled 'psychology'. Danziger (1997) presents a perceptive analysis of the political and social developments that underpinned the classification of these different parts of 'psychology' and the resulting search for common categories of discourse. This included the change of label of 'behaviour' to 'behaviour*ism*' suggesting a movement rather than an investigation of fragments. Researchers such as Ivan Pavlov (1839–1936), a Russian physiologist who conducted experiments with animals and published his ideas on the process of 'conditioning', that is, the behavioural reaction to a given stimulus, was included in this behavioural focus in terms of the developing interest in the learning process. As Danziger points out, it was as if the idea of 'conditioning' was pounced on to fill a theoretical vacuum. Pavlov himself later took issue with the idea of an adoption of an end-focused explanation, rather than a starting point for further inquiry (Pavlov, 1932). Notwithstanding these tensions, in the USA John Watson, the founding father of behaviourism, had publicly expressed (c.1910) his support for an objective behaviourist approach to psychology, as well as criticism of any part of human functioning, such as introspection, which could not be observed. In 1916 he was elected President of the American Psychological Association. By this time, mainstream psychology began to proceed without direct reference to philosophical reasoning, having turned its attention to the establishment of the discipline as a 'science'.

Increasingly, psychology was modelled on activities within the physical sciences, with an interest in the use of precise measurement and mathematical approaches in the understanding of human behaviour. As Laungani (2004) has pointed out, western psychology came to be defined as the science of human and animal behaviour, examining a wide range of human functioning, including, inter alia, cognition, memory, perception, intelligence, personality, social behaviour, group functioning and mental disorder, from a scientific perspective. Laungani also makes the point that scientific psychology came to be associated with its attention to a particular methodology, rather than its conceptual frameworks. Following Wundt, the field of psychology took an increasing turn towards defining itself as a natural science driven by an ever increasing interest in the fragmentation of human experience into the methodological language of 'variables'. As Danziger (1997) states, in relation to the deployment of this new 'metalanguage', '… it merely added a new layer of description. That layer, however, came to play a more thoroughly hegemonic role than the older framework ever did. By the 1950s use of the methodological metalanguage had virtually become mandatory in the context of psychological investigation and theorizing' (p. 158).

An example of a counter movement within the scientific frame is reflected in the work of the Gestalt psychologists all of whom were active at the beginning of the 20th century. The word Gestalt, variously translated as 'shape', 'structure' or 'whole' was introduced into psychology by the Austrian philosopher Christian von Ehrenfels (1859–1932). His original essay denigrating the reductionistic approach in favour of the combining of 'atoms' into broader structures led to the establishment of the Berlin school of Gestalt psychology and to the more recent investigation of neural networks. The leading proponents of Gestalt psychology were Max

Wertheimer (1880–1943), Kurt Koffka (1887–1941) and Wolfgang Köhler (1887–1967). These researchers were profoundly critical of the fragmentation proposed by the positivists and outlined instead a research programme based on a holistic approach which highlighted the tendency of human beings to complete representations into meaningful wholes. A key proponent of Gestalt psychology, and a central figure in the later development of Gestalt psychotherapy, was Kurt Lewin (1890–1947) who developed his ideas on field theory and the impossibility of separating the individual from the wider context. These ideas were not, however, articulated within any philosophical framework; they were conceived as a critical and opposing movement to the prevailing scientific approach of the time. They also exemplify some of the tensions that prevailed about the development of psychology as a form of natural science.

The rise of humanism

Although the power of empiricism and positivism was significant in the development of mainstream psychology as a discipline separate from philosophy, and exerted (and in our view, continues to exert) a considerable and on-going influence on the culture of the profession of psychology in the broadest sense, there were other social, literary and philosophical developments that represented a challenge to that position, and which are particularly significant for the development of the specialty of counselling psychology and the psychological therapies in general. The philosopher, Bertrand Russell (1872–1970), highlights the fact that '[f]rom the latter part of the eighteenth century to the present day, art and literature and philosophy, and even politics, have been influenced, positively or negatively, by a way of feeling which was characteristic of what, in a large sense, may be called the romantic movement' (1961, p. 651). The defining characteristic of the romantic movement was an interest in the expression of emotion, and the setting of aesthetics above utilitarian standards. It might also be regarded as a form of reclaiming a theocentric focus in an increasingly secular and fragmented world. The romantic movement raised the issue of freedom and will and the tensions between individual aspirations and social or political constraint as expressed by the well known statement of the philosopher Rousseau (1712–1778) that '[m]an is born free; and everywhere he is in chains'. These developments represented a reaction to rationalism and empiricism, and highlighted the importance of the 'self' and the power of imagination. In this movement we can see the origins of the humanistic challenge to positivistic psychology, a challenge that was supported by later philosophical developments through Kant, Hegel and later 19th century writers within the phenomenological and existentialist traditions. Kant (1724–1804) in particular, drew attention to the relationship between the perception of an object and the object itself, claiming that the object itself, the noumenon, could not be known, and that knowledge therefore resided only in the object as it appeared to us, the phenomenon. He did, however, make the point that this process of perception needed to be subject to rigorous logical inquiry. Nevertheless, these ideas paved the way for a particular focus on the nature of perceptual reality, and importantly for counselling psychology, on the nature and role of the perceiver.

Spinelli (2005) draws attention to the fact that the term 'phenomenology' was used both by Kant, as well as by Hegel and Marx, but it was not until later in the 19th century that the philosophical school known as phenomenology was formed. Edmund Husserl (1859–1938) is generally regarded as the founder of modern phenomenology, and was profoundly influenced in his thinking by an earlier philosopher and psychologist, Franz Brentano (1838–1917) who had been interested in the philosophy of mind, in particular the idea of intentionality in the relationship between the subject and the object. For Brentano, intentionality was the defining feature of mental activity (McAlister, 1976). Husserl's interest was in establishing more clearly the structure of consciousness, as well as promoting a methodology, the phenomenological method, designed to enable an examination of the structure of experience and consciousness. Of particular importance to later thinking and practice within the fields of counselling psychology and psychotherapy was the notion of the co-creation between observer and observed, an idea which lies at the heart of the phenomenological position. Phenomenology as a philosophical tradition had in fact two distinct paths which can be identified in its development. The first was the set of ideas put forward by Husserl which took the form of an analysis of the structure of consciousness. A second form, known as existential phenomenology or existentialism, came into focus through the work of Husserl's colleague, Martin Heidegger (1889–1976) who had been influenced by Kierkegaard (1813–1855) and who combined an interest in the structure of consciousness with the structure of human existence and a focus on 'being-in-the-world' (Heidegger, 1962). These ideas were subsequently developed by other writers in the existential phenomenological tradition but in slightly different ways (Blackham, 1952). For example, Sartre (1905–1980) took the view that consciousness was always in process in relation to the world and therefore a particular structure could not be pinned down – in Sartre's terms 'existence precedes essence' (Sartre, 1965). Marcel (1889–1973) took a greater interest in ethics and morality, stressing relationship and communication as key aims in life, and Merleau-Ponty (1908–1961) highlighted the embodied nature of the person's exchanges with the world (Merleau-Ponty, 1962).

These ideas, highlighting the individual's struggle and challenges in their 'thrownness' into the world and the qualities in the human being's nature of expression, intention and the reaching out for contact, represented an important strand of European humanism developed in a slightly different way within the USA where the movement of humanistic psychology is regarded as having emerged from the work of Abraham Maslow (1908–1970). A writer who linked European existentialism with the humanistic movement was James Bugental who is credited with setting out the key postulates of humanistic psychology (Bugental, 1965). These postulates covered five key aspects suggesting that human beings could not be reduced to 'components', were associated with a uniquely human context, included the capacity to have an awareness of oneself in the context of other people, had the possibility of choices and responsibilities, and had the uniquely human quality of seeking meaning, value and creativity. Maslow's emphasis on human striving and self-actualization was heralded, along with others who emphasized the importance of advancing a more holistic vision of psychology, as the third force in psychology, after behaviourism and psychoanalysis. The *Journal of Humanistic Psychology* was launched in 1961 and the Association of Humanistic Psychology was formed in 1963. In 1971 humanistic psychology was recognized by the American Psychological Association and granted its own division (Division 32). Since that time the interest in humanistic ideas has continued, reflected both in the development of the profession of counselling psychology, and currently in the 'relational' focus that is informing a number of different areas of the psychological therapies and serving to bring different approaches much closer together. Examples of these emerging fields include the focus on relational psychoanalysis (e.g. Mitchell and Aron, 1999), the recent interest in relational transactional analysis (e.g. Hargaden and Sills, 2002) and relational forms of cognitive behaviour therapy (e.g. Young, Klosko and Weishaar, 1999). We can see also that the rise of humanism took place alongside the developing interest in a number of different countries in counselling psychology as a separate field of theory and practice.

The emergence of depth psychology

From what we have covered so far, it is possible to see that we can identify a powerful movement reflected in mainstream psychology, a movement that emphasized a clear separation between its activities and any philosophical reflections – a prevailing model that had come to be based on the natural sciences. We can also see how these pursuits became enshrined in institutional settings, reflected either in university departments and laboratories, or in formal professional bodies within psychology. The rise of humanism represented a rather different set of developments with its own identity and obvious tensions with mainstream psychology. A third set of developments, yet another form of psychology, is reflected in the development of psychoanalysis by Sigmund Freud (1856–1939) and his followers in Vienna at the end of the 19th century. We can also discern the origins of these developments in earlier philosophical interests outlined above which highlighted the unconscious elements of human functioning. While never seemingly accepted into mainstream psychology the influence of Freud and his followers has been significant, not only in terms of everyday thinking – most people have heard something about Freud and will have a view to express – but also particularly in the context of the psychological therapies. By raising the issue of consciousness not being the controlling function of human activity Freud posed a significant challenge to mainstream psychology (Gay, 1995). Of course Freud's ideas were rejected by the positivists and thereafter followed an on-going struggle between the two camps with the 'scientists' interested in discrediting Freud's ideas. Notwithstanding his description of himself as an adventurer (Freud, 1960) Freud's training had been as a scientist, operating within a medical/neurological framework, and he explicitly asserted his interest in the development of a scientific psychology (Freud, 1950). Through the 'evidence' obtained in the context of his clinical work he increasingly moved towards a psychological analysis of his patients' presenting difficulties. In the context of the current emerging field of affective neuroscience (see, for example, Schore, 1994; Siegel, 1999 Schore, 2003a; Schore, 2003b) and its support for the idea of the 'unconscious' as articulated by Freud, we can perhaps view Freud's attempts at a neurological explanation of human functioning as ahead of his time. The technological advances that are currently employed within affective neuroscience were not available to Freud, which meant that he needed to turn to an alternative framework for the development of a theoretical scheme.

The evaluation of depth psychology as defined originally by Freud and his followers, varies depending on the standpoint of the observer. From the perspective of the 'scientist', especially within the formulation of science in mainstream psychology, psychoanalysis is not a science but an art. On the other hand, from the standpoint of the ordinary person, psychoanalysis speaks to a commonsense view of human behaviour. As human beings, we are not surprised by the assertion that many of our motivations are not available to conscious reflection, and can only emerge through the reflexive analysis of actions in the world. The movement of psychoanalysis has also had a significant impact on philosophical and epistemological writings in more recent times, and is thus also relevant to consider in terms of a philosophical position within the field of counselling psychology. Anthony Giddens, the social theorist, (e.g. Giddens, 1987, 1991) draws on psychoanalytic theory, specifically the theory of the unconscious, to illuminate everyday behaviour and social relations, and adds to Freud's conceptualization the idea of 'practical consciousness'. According to Giddens:

> Practical consciousness is in a certain sense unconscious. That is to say, it consists of forms of knowledge not immediately available to discourse. But it is not unconscious in the same way as symbols and modes of cognition subject to repression are unconscious. For these latter forms of cognition cannot be translated into discourse without the influence of some kind of distorting mechanism. The unconscious has a definite role in human social activity, and it is reasonable to argue that one can at least make headway in understanding what the unconscious is by following the line of thought that the unconscious 'is structured like a language'. But intervening between the unconscious and the conscious is practical consciousness, the medium of human practical activity. (1987, p. 63)

Interestingly, this concept of practical consciousness also provides a bridge to behaviourism but in a less fragmented way than has been the case in mainstream psychology. The theory of sexuality proposed by Freud is also focused on by Giddens (1991) to analyse what he terms as the 'privatising of passion', a feature of the modernist era generally taken as dating from the 1880s to about 1945.

The feminist movement provides us with an interesting example of the way in which psychoanalysis was used to critique a number of philosophical ideas (Minsky, 1996). The feminist critique focuses on the role of the masculine within philosophy and the resulting exclusion of the feminine. These arguments serve to undermine the assumed neutrality of philosophy itself, highlighting the unconscious formation of knowledge in gendered terms. Kirschner (1996) considers the psychoanalytic developmental narrative from the perspective of cultural discourse. She links the emergence of psychoanalysis to the romantic movement and the disillusionment with the industrial revolution, as well as to the progressive secularization of society where God has been relegated to a position of relative unimportance.

Homans (1989) identifies psychoanalysis as emanating from both religion and science. He highlights the origins of psychoanalysis as a response to the loss of meaningful constructions in human life, with particular emphasis on western cultural development. He directs the reader's attention:

> to the most terrible of all the historical ironies which the psychoanalytic movement presents to us: the fact that analytic access and its associated capacity to tolerate the chaos of the inner world – and through that to tolerate the chaos of the social world – emerged historically directly alongside its moral and psychological opposite, the rise of National Socialism (the politics of fantasy). (1989, p. 336)

Homans draws parallels between these two movements, with psychoanalysis demonstrating the capacity to mourn the loss of a previous worldview, and National Socialism demonstrating the incapacity to mourn. It is clear that psychoanalysis as a movement has been instrumental in promoting a wide range of modern philosophical ideas, while remaining profoundly at odds with mainstream psychology. Leahey (2004), for example, takes up a critical position, expressing disillusionment with Freud's ideas. In a discussion of Lacan's identification (1968) of Freud, Marx and Nietzsche as the three leaders of the Party of Suspicion which Lacan considers has made a significant contribution to 20th century philosophical thinking, Leahey states: 'What Freud and the Party of Suspicion have bequeathed us is paranoia' (2004, p. 294).

Social constructionism, deconstruction and the postmodern era

The 20th century has seen the development of ideas that take a critical perspective on the generation of knowledge and on a range of conceptualizations that emerged from the period of 'modernity'. These developments are concerned with challenging the belief that categories of knowledge could in fact be identified in an objective and fragmented way in terms of divorcing aspects of enquiry from their context, and that there could be a linear development of theoretical insights towards some notion of larger 'truths'. In one sense, we could think of these developments in terms of Thomas Kuhn's ideas (Kuhn, 1970) concerning the nature of scientific revolutions. Kuhn states that: 'All crises begin with the blurring of a paradigm and the consequent loosening of the rules for normal research' (1970, p. 84). He goes on to state, in the postscript to the second edition of his book, that: 'a paradigm governs, in the first instance, not a subject matter but rather a group of practitioners' (1970, p. 180). He concludes this second edition with the idea that: 'Scientific knowledge, like language, is intrinsically the common property of a group or else nothing at all' (1970, p. 210). Kuhn's emphasis on scientific knowledge as the property of a group of scientists grappling with how to arrive at an even better form of knowledge, and faced with inconsistencies in their methods, has been criticized as remaining positioned within a form of representational knowledge, leaving scientists believing that they can still find out what the truth 'really' is (Lather, 1992). At the same time we could view Kuhn's ideas as moving towards the position set out originally by Berger and Luckmann (1966) in their contextualizing of knowledge production in the social setting, and their suggestion that any exploration of knowledge requires 'an inquiry into the manner in which this reality is constructed' (1966, p. 30). It is our tacitly shared agreements about what constitutes a discourse that forms knowledge about the world. We are now in an era of this kind of questioning which at times takes the form of an annihilation of previous ideas. Referring to postmodernism, Løvlie (1992) suggests that '[i]ntellectually, it is the voice of the modern sceptic, and violently so' (p. 121).

This new era of postmodern thinking has created a culture of questioning and deconstruction of existing ideas which has posited itself as a new philosophy. This trend is evident in a large number of fields (Lyotard, 1984) focusing on art, architecture, and literature as well as psychology. The critique in psychology focuses on the sociology of knowledge and on the array of cultural and power processes on which knowledge production rests. For example, Parker et al. (1995) focus on mental health and psychopathology, highlighting the role of language as structuring both reason and unreason. Foucault (2001) has brought out the hidden power processes operating in our mental health systems, while Parker (1999) offers us a systematic deconstruction of theory and practice in psychotherapy. Derrida (1978) focused on language and text, presenting an analysis of the distinction between 'signifier' and 'signified' and suggesting that all we have is the signifier embedded in our language patterns. Essentially, Derrida articulated a self-reflexivity that appears aimed at doing away with subjectivity. The central theme of postmodernism is that the 'grand narrative' of unifying theory is not possible; since all knowledge is socially constructed, the focus needs to be on local, more boundaried concerns, with specific attention paid to contextual factors. There is currently much heated debate in this field, with many writers setting up a modernist monster to be radically deconstructed, and others wanting to accept the critical turn without throwing the baby out with the bathwater. Perhaps, as suggested by Feyerabend (1987), what is necessary is that we aim to 'go beyond empty slogans and [to] start *thinking*' (italics in the original, 1987, p. 161).

The philosophical challenge for the profession of counselling psychology

In thinking about the issues set out above, it is clear that the formation of a 'core philosophy' in counselling psychology is no easy matter. To be too radical is to depart from the home base of institutionalized mainstream psychology, symbolized by the BPS. To be too conservative is to risk minimizing just those values that counselling psychology as a profession was set up to support. These are the values of humanism and subjectivity. Even the latter idea of subjectivity is now additionally under threat from postmodern perspectives. In our view, it requires a significant level of intellectual and emotional confidence to wade through this quagmire of ideas and formulate something that presents with coherence. In our different roles within the profession of counselling psychology we have both had to negotiate a tricky path that sought to maintain a sense of our own integrity, identifying a position that held on to an intelligent standard, as well as satisfying a number of stakeholders. We have both found this journey challenging and at times stressful. We can see, however, that it is also a particularly interesting challenge, and one that is more easily tackled if we avoid an antagonistic position, going instead for a 'both/and' approach. The history of mainstream psychology represents a complex set of developments. The dream that science could answer the challenges faced by human beings was in our view understandable given the historical context. The fact that this turned out to be more complicated as a goal comes as no surprise, but it does not mean that we need to discard all of the contributions within that tradition. Likewise, human motivation, while not necessarily driven primarily by a sexual drive as suggested by Freud, needs to be approached as a multi-level phenomenon, not always available to immediate conscious exploration. We need to seek a position that can encompass a critical perspective on language and power, without losing sight of a referent. As Bekerman and Tatar (2005) point out, '… telling the counsellee that his/her pathological personality/identity is constructed and that the world that surrounds him/her (cultural context) is equally constructed will not deliver the goods of recovery' (p. 416). These writers propose an approach termed 'postpositivist realism' (Moya and Hames-Garcia, 2000) which they suggest leaves more room for an emphasis on change, while also recognizing the fact that the distribution of goods and resources is driven by labels or identities. Our own view is that in our search for a coherent philosophical position for the field of counselling psychology, we need to proceed with a certain sense of humility. As Chaiklin (1992) suggests '… most psychologists would be happy if we could understand human practices and conditions in a way that would make a modest contribution to creating humane societal conditions' (p. 204). The field of counselling psychology is now no longer a very young field – there is a growing maturity in its theories and practices, enough we think to support a more confident exploration of the philosophical domain, ensuring that a small part is played in re-connecting with our parent discipline of philosophy in a way that generates collaboration rather than competition.

3

THE PROFESSIONAL KNOWLEDGE BASE OF COUNSELLING PSYCHOLOGY

In this chapter we address a number of the specifics of counselling psychology's knowledge base as defined by the profession itself. Our previous chapter highlighted the complexity of the philosophical ideas that may be considered as a backdrop to the more overt knowledge base, as well as drawing attention to the different kinds of knowledge that result from different underlying positions. We would encourage the reader to view what is presented here with those points in mind. The Division of Counselling Psychology has articulated several different areas of knowledge that a professional in this field should have. These include: philosophical knowledge, psychological knowledge, knowledge about theoretical models in psychological therapy, knowledge about research, ethics, professional issues and practice, and reflexive knowledge derived from the undertaking of personal therapy and the experience of supervision. In the context of training courses in this profession, different institutions tend to highlight different aspects of the knowledge base, especially in relation to philosophical positions and the major psychotherapeutic traditions. As outlined later in our chapter on training, trainees on accredited courses in counselling psychology have only to demonstrate in-depth knowledge in one main approach to psychological therapy and a working knowledge of one other. This is equally the case for trainees following the 'independent route' in the UK. However, it is also true that one of the characteristics of this professional field is that it is wide ranging, and practitioners pursue their careers in a broad range of locations.

We consider that it may be useful to anyone thinking about training in this profession to have a clear understanding of the breadth and complexity of the professional knowledge involved, and to reflect on where they might want to locate themselves in the different approaches and debates. In the sections below, we review the different kinds of knowledge that are a part of this field; we focus in particular on the more overt aspects since we have already covered the philosophical domain. We present an outline of the different approaches to psychological therapy, with some emphasis on their historical development as well as on current perspectives within each tradition. We also summarize research which has evaluated these different approaches and reflect on the implications for practice. The requirement for personal psychological therapy during training adds another perspective to the concept of professional knowledge, as do the practice requirements and related supervision. A further factor that currently distinguishes counselling psychology from, for example, the professions of counselling and psychotherapy is the significant emphasis placed on research activity by professionals in the field. This raises a number of interesting issues regarding the nature of research and inquiry in counselling psychology, given the value base of the profession. The developing trend towards different forms of integration in the therapeutic field as a whole is also reviewed, and we highlight a number of ideas relevant to this trend together with related research where appropriate.

Psychological knowledge

At the heart of the profession of counselling psychology lies a broad range of knowledge that can be described as psychological, and reflecting a number of the ideas outlined in our previous chapter. These ideas are not exclusive to counselling psychology of course, and many also intertwine with those highlighted in the context of the therapeutic traditions. We consider that it is worth thinking about what might constitute the uniqueness of 'psychological knowledge' since this is an issue often raised in accreditation debates, as well as the fact that such knowledge is highlighted as a separate category within the list of competencies for the profession. We are told that we need to know about theories relevant to counselling psychology, that we should understand theories of mind and personality, understand social and cultural contexts throughout the life span, and focus on life-span development, psychopathology, testing and pharmacology. It is clear that these competencies are not the exclusive property of the field of counselling psychology, since they are as relevant to those professionals that describe themselves as psychotherapists, and who may not have a first degree in psychology. These competencies are also relevant to clinical psychologists and to psychiatrists, and we need to watch out for a tendency to colonize professional spaces (Woolfe, 2002).

Notwithstanding the difficulties of identity and boundary settings in the helping professions, we do consider that a first degree in psychology and the influence that this has on the planning of a postgraduate syllabus does provide an important base to the field. We are thinking, for example, about the wide range of ideas that the field of psychology as a whole has given us. The broad field of psychology encompasses firstly a social perspective, ranging from an analysis of power processes in society, the workings of groups and processes of influence. Secondly, psychology offers us perspectives on the physiology of human beings, the intricacies of our memory systems, general cognitive functioning and the physiological effects of stress. This kind of knowledge is crucial, for example, in dealing therapeutically with the experience of trauma. Finally, the history of psychology offers us a wide range of perspectives on developmental processes, which include ideas relevant to the life span as a whole. Many of these broad ideas underlie approaches in the different therapeutic traditions which we consider below.

The major psychotherapeutic traditions

When talking or writing about psychotherapeutic traditions, we mostly find reference to three broad approaches: the psychoanalytic-psychodynamic, the cognitive-behavioural, and the humanistic-existential. While Spinelli (1994) argues for the existence of four traditions, separating the humanistic from the existential-phenomenological, our preference is for remaining with the focus on the original three as outlined above. In reality, each of these traditions encompasses many different kinds of therapeutic approaches, and across all three we often find some overlap within specific therapeutic modalities. It is worth remembering also that Kazdin (1986) identified over 400 different types of therapy! In any case, these three categories provide us with a starting point for exploration, and each conveys a richness and developmental trajectory of its own. A few key principles are worth outlining in terms of these three traditions, at least as viewed as separate historical entities. Firstly, each differs to some extent in the view taken of the human being, the assumptions made about what factors contribute to the development of the person, and the factors that predispose to psychological difficulties. Secondly, in their origins, different perspectives on what constitutes human motivation may be discerned. Thirdly, the theories of change in which each is embedded are different; and finally, the role of the therapist differs in each of these approaches in terms of the methodologies adopted. It should also be noted that the traditions outlined below may be adapted for work with individuals, groups or systems.

The psychoanalytic-psychodynamic tradition

As we have seen from our previous chapter, the psychoanalytic approach was originally set out and developed by Freud and his colleagues at the end of the 19th century. Freud expanded his approach over a period of time as different ideas came to him in the course of treating his patients; it is possible, therefore, to discern contradictions and changes of mind in his ideas as they unfold in his writings. The language of psychoanalysis as it was elaborated reflected the medical context and related cause and effect model in which it was embedded. The patient consulted the doctor who remained very much the expert, and in Freud's case also, the scientist. Freud articulated a number of key theoretical ideas which form the foundations of the psychoanalytic approach.

One key concept was the idea of the unconscious, the notion that certain aspects of experience could not be directly accessed by the person. While the idea of the unconscious had been around before Freud, he was certainly instrumental in popularizing this notion, both within and outside the therapeutic community. According to Freud, personality is the expression of a balance of intrapsychic forces, and the balance of these forces at any one time would be likely to have behavioural consequences. These forces are driven by the different needs of the id, ego and superego, what Freud (1949) called 'the psychical apparatus'. Freud viewed intrapsychic life as containing significant amounts of conflict, usually derived from early experience, and susceptible to re-enactment in the present – what Freud highlighted as the pull towards repetition. In order to cope with intrapsychic conflicts, a process which Freud viewed as applying to all people, not just to his patients, a person needs to draw on a number of defences which have the function of keeping the more difficult conflicts outside of conscious reflection. Key defence mechanisms identified included the processes of repression, denial, projection, introjection, reaction formation, rationalization, reversal and displacement. The most difficult conflicts were viewed by Freud as having to do with sexual drives and primitive instincts. On the basis of the material presented to him by his patients, Freud formulated his theory of infantile sexuality and posited the Oedipus complex as the constellation which lay at the heart of psychological difficulties. On the basis of his clinical experiences, and the ways in which early unresolved difficulties re-emerged in the course of treatment, Freud formulated his ideas of transference and countertransference, concepts which are key to the technique of psychoanalysis. The psychotherapeutic process involves the analyst adopting an attitude of 'evenly-hovering attention' (Freud, 1912) as the analysand allows her or himself to free associate, or to report on dreams, in order to find out what might emerge from the unconscious realm of experience. There is also a focus on the elements of that experience which could be identified as being transferred into the present relational space between analyst and patient. The analyst's role is to carefully monitor their own affective responses to emerging forms of exchange as potential sources of information about unconscious processes, to offer interpretations of material expressed by the patient, and to work directly with the patient's defences as expressed through the dynamics of the transference relationship. Sandler, Dare and Holder (1992) provide a comprehensive overview of the psychoanalytic process, including the many ways that the basic concepts have evolved, even through Freud's own working life.

While many of the core ideas outlined above remain important within subsequent traditions that evolved from psychoanalysis, a number of different schools have developed since Freud's original formulations. Alfred Adler (1870–1937) broke away from Freud's group quite early on, developing an approach known as individual psychology. He emphasized the holistic nature of the person in their context and the consistent unity of the self (Clifford, 1996). Carl Jung (1875–1961) disagreed with Freud about the nature of the unconscious and developed his own school of thought which he called analytical psychology. He postulated that a part of the unconscious included a set of universal patterns which he termed archetypes, and which are inherited from the 'collective unconscious'. Heinz Hartmann (1894–1970) became particularly interested in the function of the ego and was the founder of what came to be known as ego-psychology. He focused on the idea of a conflict-free part of the ego, shifting significantly the earlier intrapsychic dynamic proposed by Freud. Melanie Klein (1882–1960) focused specifically on the first year of life and postulated a developmental scheme during this period. She also introduced the concept of projective identification, a concept that has since been developed by several writers (e.g. Sandler, 1989; Ogden, 1992) and which is also of current interest within neuroscientific research (Schore, 2003b). Melanie Klein was also the first analyst to focus specifically on a person's need to relate to 'objects', an idea that was later developed by theorists such as Fairbairn, Balint, Winnicott and Guntrip, key theorists in what is known as the British Object Relations school, and by writers such as Sullivan, Masterson and Kernberg in the USA. These writers focused on the relational needs of the individual and began to challenge the idea of a one-person psychology as well as the classical drive theory proposed by Freud (see, for example, Greenberg and Mitchell, 1983; Gomez, 1997).

John Bowlby (1907–1990) also developed his ideas within the object relations tradition although his ideas gained an independent theoretical focus. Bowlby's focus was on the relationship of the infant to their primary care-giver; his ideas came to be referred to as attachment theory, a theory which has since been taken forward by many contemporary writers and researchers. Eric Berne (1910–1970) moved away from psychoanalysis to develop transactional analysis psychotherapy (Berne, 1986), an approach that brought a reformulated language to intrapsychic and interpersonal processes and a more structured approach to treatment. Jacques Lacan (1901–1981) proposed a critique and re-evaluation of Freud's writing in terms of a structural-linguistic paradigm, drawing also on philosophy and mathematics (Lacan, 1977). Heinz Kohut (1913–1981) was interested in the development of healthy relational needs and formulated a set of theoretical ideas known as self psychology. He focused on the importance of empathy in the exchange between analyst and patient, proposing the concept of self-object transferences which reflected the human being's need to be mirrored, to idealize and to recognize themselves in another. These ideas paved the way for the later development of intersubjectivity theory (Stolorow, Atwood and Ross, 1978; Stolorow and Atwood, 1992) with its emphasis on the interplay between transference and countertransference in the relational exchanges between patient and analyst. The focus, therefore, moved towards an exploration of the intersubjective field and the system of reciprocal mutual influence (Beebe and Lachmann, 2002) at both conscious and unconscious levels of exchange.

As these developments unfolded, the term 'psychodynamic' became commonplace in talking about an approach that was interested in depth perspectives on the person in relationship, and related ideas for therapeutic practice. As Jacobs (1988) points out '[g]iven the different theories that have developed from and within psychoanalysis, the word "psychodynamic" is a useful one since it encompasses the different schools …' (p. 4). According to Jacobs the purpose of a psychodynamic approach, regardless of the particular theoretical orientation, is to make the unconscious conscious, thereby providing the client with some new insights, a broader awareness, and increased control over choices and decisions. The overall purpose is to understand the past in the present (Jacobs, 1986). Kahn (1991) emphasizes the coming together of early psychoanalysis with a more humanistic attitude and an acceptance that the analyst cannot be a blank screen and must be willing to participate in the exchange between therapist and client. This idea is key to current developments in the field and remains important however much some current writers might argue and disagree. Two of the more recent strands of development are represented by 'intersubjectivity theory' and 'relational psychoanalysis', with both strands concerned to recognize the existence of two subjectivities in the therapeutic encounter, and a commitment to a two-person psychology. Some writers such as DeYoung (2003) take a broad perspective and argue that the two approaches have more commonalities than differences. At the same time, she places herself within the intersubjective stream. Perhaps, as Maroda (1998) suggests, in the context of a discussion about theoreticians perceiving the world of their approach from the perspective of their own early stories and experiences, 'rather than gossiping about the early determinants of Jung's or Adler's or Freud's or Lacan's theories, I think we are ahead in *assuming* that what any one of us says about the human condition is, at best, true of ourselves, and, at worst, a defence against what is true of ourselves' (p. 7, italics in original). This idea is echoed in a review by Beebe et al. (2005), who make the point that each theorist brings a different lens developed through their own history to the framing of what is important in the therapeutic exchange. Also, it is evident that the language of both intersubjectivity and relationality as applied to psychoanalysis is brought together in a variety of writings (e.g. Mitchell, 2000). A number of current writers in the psychoanalytic tradition, such as Mills (2005), draw attention also to various contradictions and shortcomings in these developing ideas, while welcoming the advent of a less technique-driven approach to the psychoanalytic field as a whole.

The cognitive-behavioural tradition

As we have seen from the previous chapter, the origins of behaviourism lie in the development of mainstream psychology, with its interest in seeking out a scientific basis to the profession modelled on the natural sciences. John Watson (1878–1958) in particular had set out the overarching goal of psychology as an objective science, with no room for anything that could not be directly observed. A key early idea in the development of behaviourism was the aligning of human research with animal research. While some dissenting voices argued for the on-going exploration of consciousness as an important part of psychology, the rise of behaviourism was politically supported by the power of institutionalized psychology and the fact that, for example, in 1916 Watson became president of the American Psychological Association (APA). By the 1950s behaviourism had taken hold in the profession, emphasizing the effects of learning and the behavioural consequences of conditioning. As Leahey (2004) points out, there were many different forms of behaviourism. However, one of the best known approaches is the radical behaviourism proposed by B. F. Skinner (1904–1990) who advocated the experimental analysis of the conditioning process. This took the focus away from 'persons', towards the contingencies of reinforcement in learning terms, and the investigation of stimuli and responses. The language of 'variables' was utilized in the experimental analysis of antecedent independent variables and the consequent dependent variables. This evolving field discriminated between 'reflex' responses to a stimulus and 'operant' responses where the animal learned, for example, to press a lever to avoid shock or gain food. Skinner even turned his attention to language as behaviourally based (Skinner, 1957) suggesting that the constellation of stimulus, response and reinforcement were key to a child's learning of language, where words became behavioural sounds emitted as a result of reinforcement by a parent.

The behavioural approach was brought into the therapeutic domain by Arnold Lazarus, a South African psychotherapist who developed his ideas in the context of his own practice and who later, together with Joseph Wolpe, published a key book setting out some of the principles of his behavioural approach and its application to the therapeutic setting (Wolpe and Lazarus, 1966). Some of the language of behaviour therapy, such as 'maladjusted' versus 'well adjusted', found its way into a range of settings and inevitably created confusion regarding a behavioural versus a person focus. An example of this can be found in a research project that one of us (Vanja) undertook in the 1970s in a school for 'maladjusted' children, a term which kept the focus on children's behaviours rather than on the very disadvantaged conditions in which these children had developed, and their resulting perceptions of the world. Lazarus, however, came to recognize his behavioural focus as being somewhat limited within the therapeutic setting (Lazarus, 1971) and laid the foundations for cognitive-behaviour therapy in the development of his broad spectrum multimodal therapy (Lazarus, 1976). Albert Bandura was also a key figure in the expansion of a behavioural perspective and proposed his social learning theory which focused on the reciprocal determinism of the environment and behaviour (Bandura, 1977). These developments led to a greater interest in the roles of perception and expectation in the learning process and hence to a therapeutic interest in how these factors could be harnessed to bring about change in a client. George Kelly, for example, developed personal construct theory on the basis of a constructivist philosophy emphasizing the meaning-making capabilities of human beings and highlighting a person's anticipation of events in the world based on how the world was being construed (Kelly, 1963). He was strongly opposed to the medical model and the identification of psychological 'illness' (Fransella and Dalton, 1996), favouring instead an attitude that views the human being as a scientist, capable of inquiring into their constructions, predictions and resulting behaviours.

Probably two of the best known names associated directly with cognitive behaviour therapy (CBT) are Albert Ellis and Aaron Beck, both of whom interestingly had a background in psychoanalysis. Ellis (1913–2007) was a clinical psychologist and is often regarded as the grandfather of CBT, with Beck as father. Ellis' approach promoted a focus on thinking, action and outcome rather than on past influences, and on the interaction between cognitive, emotional and behavioural factors as a focus for the psychotherapist. He developed what he initially called Rational-Emotive Therapy (Ellis and Whiteley, 1979), and which he later re-named Rational Emotive Behaviour Therapy (REBT) in response to critics who had accused him of playing down the highlighting of behaviour in favour of cognition and emotion (Dryden, 1996). However, a key assumption of this position is the tendency of human beings to be constructivist in their perceptions highlighting the meaning that a person might place on a situation or event. Following on from this idea, if a person's perceptions of a given situation or event could be changed, then emotional and behavioural consequences would follow. Ellis proposed that human beings had two competing tendencies. Firstly, he viewed the person as essentially motivated to look for happiness. At the same time, he viewed the person as having a biological tendency to become irrational and disturbed (Ellis, 1976). Through an active exploration of cognitive constructions, human beings would have the opportunity of fulfilling the tendency towards happiness and not the tendency towards irrationality. One interesting aspect of Ellis's framework is that it does not necessarily need to be located within a therapeutic setting. His writings offer a self-help approach to therapeutic change (see, for example, Ellis and Harper, 1975).

Although Aaron Beck had undergone training in psychoanalysis as well as using that approach in the clinical setting, his early professional background had been in medicine and psychiatry and his scientific interest was in investigating more serious disturbances which presented in the psychiatric setting. He thus began a series of studies into depression and concluded that thinking played a key part in the experiences of depressed patients (Beck, 1963, 1964). He noticed that these patients tended to present with a series of automatic negative thoughts which often seemed to appear out of nowhere. These thoughts had a generalizing quality and focused on the person themselves, his/her world, and the future. This research led Beck to re-think some of the concepts that he had taken on through his training in psychoanalysis and to re-formulate his ideas towards a different kind of approach based on an exploration of the cognitive elements of the depressed person's world (Beck, 1972). He also focused on the underlying beliefs and assumptions that were instrumental in keeping certain automatic thought processes in place. These included a consideration of logical errors such as the tendency to generalize from small pieces of information, magnifying or minimizing events or information, taking issues personally when the information does not warrant it, and the tendency to engage in dichotomous thinking such a 'good' or 'bad' with a particular interest in the negative polarity. Beck also had an interest in psychometrics and the Beck Depression Inventory (BDI) is one of the most widely used instruments for the measurement of depression. He emphasized the careful conceptualization of presenting problems in scientific terms so as to enable the clinician to be as focused and specific as possible in the development of a treatment plan. Beck's ideas became particularly influential in the profession of clinical psychology, especially in the UK, and all National Health Service mental health settings will be familiar with these ideas.

The cognitive-behavioural approach has developed since Beck's early formulations in a number of different ways. One key element supporting these developments was the recognition that personality factors could underpin, for example, a tendency to depression, and both Beck and other writers and researchers have developed this idea, formulating approaches for dealing with the structures of personality as defined by the Diagnostic and Statistical Manual of Mental Disorders (American Psychiatric Association, 2000). This has led to a focus on underlying patterns of thinking and emotion, referred to as schema, and clearer formulations with regard to assessment and intervention for different presenting problems (e.g. Young, 1999; Simos, 2002; Beck et al., 2003). We have also seen the development of forms of cognitive behavioural therapy which take into account the needs of particular client groups (e.g. the dialectical behaviour therapy of Linehan, 1993), and approaches which integrate ideas from other modalities (e.g. Schema Therapy, Young, Klosko and Weishaar, 2003; Cognitive Analytic Therapy, Ryle and Kerr, 2002; Experiential Psychotherapy, Greenberg, Watson and Lietaer, 1999; Mindfulness-Based Cognitive Therapy, Segal, Williams and Teasdale, 2002). Whereas originally conceived as a short-term approach to therapy with a practical focus in terms of outcome, the different forms of this approach now cover a wide range of presenting problems from the less serious to the highly disturbed, with the focus also on treatments of different time lengths. The particular interest of many practitioners in a research-based approach has placed cognitive behaviour therapy in a very strong position politically in terms of the needs of service providers such as the National Health Service, as well as in the gaining of research grants. A more broad-based movement, emanating from the traditions of clinical psychology and cognitive behaviour therapy but with a humanistically driven philosophical base, is the movement of positive psychology (Seligman, 2002; Seligman et al., 2005). Seligman and his colleagues in this movement take issue with the traditional focus on ill health, suffering and disorder in psychology, suggesting a revised focus on the study of optimal human functioning. The aim overall is to increase happiness in individuals and institutions, defined by an empirically oriented approach to the identification of positive emotions, positive character traits and enabling institutions.

The humanistic-existential tradition

The humanistic movement, heralded as the 'third force' in psychology, developed in the 1950s as a reaction against both behaviourism and psychoanalysis. The climate was right for this emergence in the spirit of post-war economic expansion and the move towards more liberated values. The founding of the *Journal of Humanistic Psychology* in 1961 and the formation of the Association of Humanistic Psychology (AHP) in 1963 were particularly significant developments. We have also seen the way that European versions of humanism within the existentialist tradition came together with American versions in the work of James Bugental (Bugental, 1965) and his five key postulates of humanistic psychology. While we acknowledge the broad range of ideas offered in this particular tradition, leading to many different kinds of approaches within humanistic therapy, our view is that the movement as a whole is too important to separate out the humanistic from the existential-phenomenological, even if this leaves us with a consideration of a very wide range of ways of approaching therapeutic activities. Many key figures associated with different types of approaches in practice identified themselves as part of the broad humanistic movement. This included Abraham Maslow, Carl Rogers, Clark Moustakis, Rollo May, Kurt Goldstein, Fritz Perls, R. D. Laing and James Bugental among others. What these writers and therapists had in common was an emphasis on the 'ordinariness' of the human being in the world, the everyday concerns about life, death, hope, love, relating, being and making meaning.

The emphasis was not on illness as per the medical model, nor on theoretically derived concepts of intrapsychic life, but on people's existence in the world and their aspirations for belonging, contact and health – all the key elements that point to what it means to be human. While there are many differently named therapies within this tradition, we propose to highlight four key approaches which we believe cover the central tenets of humanism, yet which have different forms of theoretical expression and, to some extent, different forms of practice associated with each. At the same time, each is concerned with the creation of meaning, with a holistic view of the person in process, with phenomenological experience, and with authentic dialogue in the present. We shall consider in turn the person-centred approach, the Gestalt approach, existential psychotherapy and transpersonal psychotherapy.

Person centred approach

Carl Rogers (1902–1987) was the founder of client centred therapy which he later renamed as the person centred approach in recognition of the application of his ideas to settings beyond therapy. He was a clinical psychologist who had been deeply influenced by John Dewey's philosophy of education and the importance of the person being involved experientially in learning within a democratic environment. Rogers postulated that the human being had a tendency to grow towards health, a tendency that was on-going through life. He called this the actualizing tendency. He suggested that certain conditions would be likely to support this tendency, particularly the experience of being understood, seen, accepted and validated within a relational context. In his 'nineteen propositions' he set out his views on human functioning, the nature of change and development, and the conditions under which actualization might occur (Rogers, 1951). Rogers described seven stages of process towards optimal development, a process that involved opening oneself to the full existential possibilities of life. When these stages are fulfilled, then the person's self-concept will be functioning in the healthiest way; where a person is engaged with on a 'conditional' basis, then their self-concept will suffer and the person will experience incongruence in their sense of self. In the therapeutic setting, Rogers proposed six relational conditions based on unconditional acceptance by the therapist and the authentic nature of the exchange which would support the client to move through the seven stages of process towards fulfilment. In his writings, Rogers explicitly refers to existential living and the importance of the 'now' moment (Rogers, 1961, p. 188), and his interest in phenomenology extended also to the research setting (e.g. Kirschenbaum and Henderson, 1990). Rogers' ideas play a significant part in many humanistic counselling and psychotherapy trainings since they articulate some of the core skills required within the therapeutic context; they also remain influential in their own right.

The Gestalt approach

Gestalt psychotherapy was founded by Fritz Perls (1893–1970), a psychiatrist and psychoanalyst born in Germany of Jewish descent. Together with his wife, Laura Perls, he challenged some of the orthodoxy of psychoanalysis, proposing a more holistic approach based not only on intrapsychic processes but also on the body, biological processes and behaviour (Perls, Hefferline and Goodman, 1951). It was reportedly during his experience of being in analysis with Wilhelm Reich that he developed the concept of organismic self-regulation which was later to become one of the central tenets of Gestalt psychotherapy (Woldt and Toman, 2005), along with a focus on awareness, phenomenology and contact. The Gestalt psychologists referred to in our earlier chapter were also relevant in contributing ideas of human perception, the desire for completion and the principle of figure and ground. The rise of fascism in Germany meant that Perls and some of his collaborators had to flee the country. Perls initially fled to South Africa and later settled in the USA where the anarchic roots of his approach came into conflict with establishment thinking as defined by the professional specialties of the American Psychological Association (APA). Nonetheless, his approach became very well known among a wide range of thinkers, writers and lay people and he was accorded a central place in the human potential movement. The Gestalt approach is rooted in the notion of the flow of energy or experience in the context of self-regulation, and the need for individuals to expand their awareness so that this creative energetic flow can move unimpeded by 'interruptions' or 'moderations' through an on-going set of developmental cycles. These ideas drew also on traditions within Zen Buddhism, existentialism and psychodrama. Together they pointed to a radical perspective on the notion of 'self', a self that is formed at the contact boundary with the environmental 'other' in a continuous fashion throughout life. Interestingly, these ideas are now increasingly supported by the advent of recent research in the neurosciences and infant observation studies (e.g. Stern, 2003). Important also is the idea of the inseparable nature of person and context as articulated in Kurt Lewin's field theoretical approach (see Gold, 1999, for a selection of Lewin's writings). Gestalt psychotherapy has evolved from a more exclusive focus on active experiment such as 'two chair work' to a more dialogical phenomenological position emphasizing the expansion of awareness through the relational space of the here and now.

Existential psychotherapy

The roots of existential psychotherapy lie in the philosophical ideas of Søren Kierkegaard (1813–1855) whose writings present us with a set of musings on self-determination, agency and action (for example, see Thompson, 1974). The writings of Friedrich Nietzsche (1844–1900) are also important, highlighting the existential and ethical conflicts which confront the human being as expressed through his own life and development (e.g. Russell, 1961). Rollo May's publication of his book *Existence* in 1958 supported the development of existential psychotherapy within the USA where many existentially minded therapists had become dissatisfied with the limitations of the choice of either behaviourism or psychoanalysis. A later key figure in the USA was Irvin Yalom who talks about existential psychotherapy as a dynamic approach which focuses on four central concerns that are rooted in individual existence, namely death, freedom, existential isolation and meaninglessness (Yalom, 1980). The therapeutic work involves focusing on the conscious and unconscious fears, motives, conflicts, and challenges that are raised for the individual in the tackling of these issues. Words that characterize this approach are authenticity, being in good faith, encounter, responsibility, and choice. As with the other therapeutic modalities within the humanistic tradition, a phenomenological approach is key to all exploration, highlighting the construction of meanings that we as human beings bring to our existence in the world. The approach is concerned to take a 'deep' perspective on the challenges of being human, a perspective which does not depend on any particular developmental theory, nor on a concept of linear time. As Cohn (1997) points out '[t]he existential concept of time sees past, present and future not in linear succession but as multidimensional. The past is still present in a present that anticipates the future' (p. 26). Van Deurzen-Smith (1988) highlights the way that this approach contrasts with the medical model, emphasizing reflections on life and the living of life as an art form. Spinelli (2001a, 2007) draws attention to the challenge that this approach presents to more orthodox therapeutic approaches since it reconsiders the actual nature of the therapeutic enterprise. There are now a number of different approaches outlined within the existential tradition, with the highlighting of both a USA and a British School (Cooper, 2003).

Transpersonal psychotherapy

Transpersonal psychotherapy takes the position that there are a number of experiences to do with being human that cannot adequately be explained by a reductionist approach. To quote Shakespeare's Hamlet, '[t]here are more things in heaven and earth, Horatio, [t]han are dreamt of in your philosophy'. This approach draws on a wide number of writers and practitioners, which include some of the writings of Carl Rogers, as well as others from the existentialist tradition. Although the use of the term 'transpersonal' can be traced back to William James the introduction of the term is generally associated with Abraham Maslow and his colleagues who founded the *Journal of Transpersonal Psychology* in 1969. Overall, this approach is concerned with theoretical ideas and practices that take the focus away from the ego; this does not mean a denial of the ego but rather a recognition of wider connectedness. These ideas can sometimes sit a bit uneasily in the context of mainstream psychology; yet, what is also true is that clients who come to us are generally busy with some form of 'disconnection' within themselves and with the world. These ideas also challenge the individual reductionism of many of our psychotherapeutic theories, a fact that raises issues about cultural comparison and the 'individual' as a white western construction (Pilgrim, 1997). The field of transpersonal psychotherapy covers a wide range of writers on this subject area, all of whom make their own unique contribution. The work of Carl Jung within the psychoanalytic tradition offers us reflections on the collective unconscious and the intergenerational transmission of archetypes (Jung, 1969). Roberto Assagioli (1975, 1976) formulated a particular approach known as psychosynthesis which brings the human psyche and the concept of the collective unconscious together into one conceptual framework. Other perspectives are provided by Buddhist philosophy and Zen practice (Brazier, 1995; Epstein, 1996). Martin Buber (1970) and Merleau-Ponty (1962) offer perspectives on 'the between', whereas Ken Wilber more recently locates his approach within the postmodern tradition (Wilber, 2006). John Rowan (2005) provides a good overview of the transpersonal approach, and includes both theoretical ideas and some of the related practices derived from sacred psychology. While these ideas have yet to take a central place in the field of counselling psychology, they offer a powerful critique of a more fragmented and reductionist thought process in mainstream psychology.

Research and therapeutic outcomes

A research attitude and a commitment to research activity is a key feature of the professional knowledge base of counselling psychology.

However, approaches to research in the field of counselling psychology carry a number of tensions based in the difficulties of aligning a more positivist approach with humanistic and intersubjective concerns. There is also an on-going tension between research and practice, an issue which more generally pervades the helping professions and which is increasingly being addressed in the research literature. Roth and Fonagy (2005) inter alia draw attention to the important distinction between *efficacy* studies which highlight results achieved in the context of specifically constructed research trials, and *effectiveness* in routine clinical practice. These domains are very different in terms of the aims and the strategies adopted, and some of the tensions which arise from this are summarized below. Political factors are also relevant to what is researched and how the research is undertaken, with the recent emphasis both in the USA and the UK on managed care and service delivery options having a key influence (Lambert and Ogles, 2004; Barkham, 2007). Of importance also in terms of the field of counselling psychology is the fact that we need to take an interdisciplinary perspective in attempting to evaluate what we do with our clients. It is interesting to note, for example, that important research on the outcomes of therapy are generally located within the discipline of 'psychotherapy' rather than in counselling or clinical psychology, thus blurring the boundaries of identity. At the same time, many of the researchers engaged with psychotherapeutic outcome are psychologists. In the following sections we summarize some of the research studies on the outcomes of therapy in order both to highlight the results themselves and their implications for the profession of counselling psychology, and also to demonstrate the kinds of debates that engage a professional in this field.

Since Eysenck first posed his challenge to the effectiveness of psychotherapy (Eysenck, 1952) we have seen an increasing expansion of research activity in the field. Michael Barkham highlights different 'generations' of research activity, each with its own focus (Barkham, 2007). In terms of the efficacy question, some key studies are generally cited. These are review studies collated through the methodology of meta-analysis and providing indicators of the relative effectiveness of different approaches, as well as the results achieved with different patient populations in terms of presenting problems. Key early studies using the meta-analysis methodology consistently reported the overall effectiveness of psychotherapeutic approaches when compared with non-treatment control groups (Smith and Glass, 1977; Smith, Glass and Miller, 1980). Given the predisposition to argument since Eysenck's first challenge, these results were of course criticized. This prompted a further spate of studies which sought to validate earlier review findings. Most writers draw attention to some of the methodological difficulties in the earlier review studies undertaken, with Lambert and Ogles (2004) citing studies that have replicated the earlier reviews and have as a result come up with somewhat smaller effect sizes. However, well regarded replication studies such as those undertaken by Andrews and Harvey (1981) and Landman and Dawes (1982) appeared to settle the debate for a while, with the conclusion that the positive effects of therapeutic endeavours had been supported. As Wampold (2001) points out, 'the efficacy of psychotherapy has now been firmly established and is no longer the subject of debate' (p. 59), referring consistently to an average effect size of .80.

Notwithstanding the good results from these studies in terms of the specific methodological framework adopted, their shortcomings with regard to wider methodological issues have also been highlighted. Meta-analysis is a methodology which relies on specific criteria, namely the adoption of the randomized controlled trial (RCT), where research participants are randomly allocated to treatment or control conditions, either with a view to comparing general outcomes, comparisons between different modalities, or effects in relation to different presenting issues. Attrition rates can affect the internal validity of studies, and the overall quality of different studies can also vary. In this kind of research there is an emphasis on the manualization of treatments, controls for therapist experience, symptom severity etc. in order to create conditions for relevant comparison. The number of sessions covered in the research is fixed and on the low side in order to facilitate the overall length of a study and to include a follow-up, which could be anything from three months to over a year. Journals that publish these studies are committed to this kind of positivistic paradigm in terms of the kinds of reviews that are deemed acceptable for publication. This kind of research is also upheld within health service settings which promote a commitment to evidence-based practice (EBP) and empirically supported treatment (ESTs). Norcross, Beutler and Levant (2006) provide a well argued and critical review of these developments, highlighting some of the power processes that are embedded in these approaches. They make the point that: 'At first blush, there is universal agreement that we should use evidence as a guide in determining what works. It's like publicly prizing Mother and apple pie. Can anyone seriously advocate the reverse: non evidence-based practice?' (p. 7). They go on to highlight the complexities in relation to definitions of 'evidence', the question of who does the defining of this concept, the power processes that are acted out and the practical consequences.

They invoke two injunctions of William James to do with the need for humility and the idea that assumptions are only provisional, attitudes which do not always maintain a high profile in current professional arguments. We consider that the order of words here is significant. For example, if we use the term 'practice-based evidence' we signify a different philosophy and point to a number of challenges to a more positivistic methodological framework.

Martin Seligman (1995) also adopts a critical perspective on the traditional approach to efficacy studies, suggesting that '[t]he efficacy study is the wrong method for empirically validating psychotherapy as it is actually done, because it omits too many crucial elements of what is done in the field' (p. 966). Seligman draws attention to the very different nature of the practice-based field, highlighting differences such as the lack of fixed duration of treatment, the 'active shopping' that a client typically engages in, the focus in the improvement of general functioning rather than specific symptoms, and the existence of multiple presenting problems. He suggests a greater focus on survey methodology and presents data from a large-scale USA survey based on reports from consumers of therapy. Some key outcomes of this study included: overall, treatments were effective; there was no difference between different modalities; long-term therapy produced better results; in the short term, family doctors did as well as therapists but not in the long term. The strengths of this kind of study is that it samples therapeutic activity as it occurs in the practice field, and also involves more directly the perceptions of the clients. Seligman also highlighted a number of common factors that emerged as important. These included the active expectation on the part of clients that therapy could make a difference, the rapport of alliance between therapist and client, and the empathic attunement that is part of the therapeutic process.

In relation to the relative efficacy of different therapeutic approaches, one of the earliest studies to conclude that there were no significant differences between different approaches to therapy was carried out by Rosenzweig (1936) who concluded that 'everyone has won and all must have prizes'. Drawing on *Alice in Wonderland*, Rosenzweig referred to this as 'the Dodo Bird effect', suggesting that we should be investigating common factors in therapeutic endeavours. Later more sophisticated studies such as Luborsky, Singer and Luborsky (1975) and Wampold, Mondin, Moody, Stich, Benson and Ahn (1997) have confirmed the Dodo Bird conclusion, prompting an increasing interest in those common factors or active ingredients that make the difference regardless of modality. As early as 1961 Frank and Frank had articulated a number of general healing factors which included the emotional relationship between therapist and client, the socially sanctioned role of the therapist and its power to engender hope, the explanatory rationale embedded in the process, and the prescribed procedures or rituals for the resolution of a difficulty. It is interesting to observe a return to this type of thinking in the context of research studies. A recent research focus highlights the importance of process variables that underlie therapeutic activity. These include therapist qualities and the effects of these on outcome (Luborsky, McClellan, Woody, O'Brien and Auerbach, 1985; Crits-Christoph and Mintz, 1991); the effects of training (Stein and Lambert, 1995); the importance of the therapeutic alliance (Safran and Muran, 2000) and the role of client emotional experiencing (Castonguay, Goldfried, Wiser and Rane, 1996). Lambert and Ogles (2004) group common factors into three categories: support factors, learning factors and action factors, and conclude that 'based on a review of the evidence, it appears that factors common across treatments are accounting for a substantial amount of improvement found in psychotherapy patients. These so-called common factors may even account for most of the gains that result from psychological interventions' (p. 172). An increasing number of writers and researchers are taking these ideas forward in a variety of ways, seeking to articulate these factors in more detail and to assess their impact on both the overall outcome of therapy as well as the moment-by-moment process as it unfolds over time (e.g. Greenberg, Rice and Elliot, 1993; Lambert and Barley, 2002; Jørgensen, 2004).

The research reviewed above offers considerable support to the field of counselling psychology in terms of the freedom to incorporate a variety of approaches in its training programmes and the support also to argue the case for this variety in the field. It also demands of the professional to commit themselves to understand the complexities of some of these research debates and to engage with them at both philosophical and technical levels. We recognize also that the issue of what works in the therapeutic endeavour is both an academic and a political one. We return to the political issues in our final chapter where we consider the areas of power, research and practice in more detail in the context of current debates in the UK on the statutory regulation of the helping professions.

Reflexivity and ethics

One aspect of counselling psychology which sets it apart from the other specialities within the BPS is the requirement during training to undertake personal psychological therapy. While different accredited courses stipulate different amounts of therapy the underlying value is concerned with a commitment to reflexivity. Reflexivity is concerned with an awareness of the observer as a participant in any activity, either in the therapy room with the client or as a researcher. McLeod (2001) defines reflexivity as a capacity for 'turning back one's awareness on oneself' (p. 195) thus pointing to the development of skill in the active use of the self. This is a radical idea which challenges orthodoxies in research activities, pointing towards a more relative conception of 'truth' (Alvesson and Sköldberg, 2000; Etherington, 2004). McLeod (2001) highlights three principles that follow from this emphasis on reflexivity. These include the need for a focus on the moral dimension of research; a consideration of the processes through which text is co-constructed; and the necessity for new approaches to the communication of research findings (p. 196). These ideas point to a radical element in the professional knowledge base of counselling psychology and demand of the professional an exploration of their own value base and the tacit dimensions of thinking and practice (Polanyi, 1967). Here we are in the realm of questioning an assumed valid knowledge of what constitutes a 'problem', the assumed possibility of certainty, and the belief that there is something 'out there' to be discovered. It demands that we view all knowledge as embodied and contextual, and a view of language as not being neutral. Writers such as Shotter (1992) and Fleck (1979) identify the 'traps' that researchers and practitioners can fall into in the process by which 'reality' becomes confirmed.

The active participation in the idea of the social construction of knowledge is a key element in counselling psychology. This also supports some of the important recent developments in our thinking about ethics. Both the BPS and BACP have evolved a set of principles to guide practice and research activities, representing a significant change in the formulation and management of ethical ideas and related practice, and taking us into the 'ethics as process' domain. As the BPS Code (2006) points out '[p]sychologists are likely to need to make decisions in difficult, changing and unclear situations' (p. 5), and '[m]oral principles and the codes which spell out their applications can only be guidelines for thinking about the decisions individuals need to make in specific cases' (p. 6). The practitioner now needs to think about the principles involved and is likely to be faced more directly with the complexity of such decision making and the fact that it is often impossible to identify a clear cut rule about a given situation. Thus, ethical challenges need to be fully explored with the acceptance that there may be no one best way to proceed in a given situation (Orlans, 2007). Sampson (1998) also draws attention to the ethical dimension of knowledge production and provides a critical and personal review of the challenges of embodied discourse concluding with the call for 'a movement and a political commitment directed towards challenging a history in which the denial of embodied differences has been employed more often to destroy than to nurture humanity' (p. 31).

Framing professional knowledge in counselling psychology

As we have attempted to demonstrate, certain tensions are evident in the different forms of knowledge that are a part of this profession. We would suggest that one of the factors that makes the field of counselling psychology so distinctive is the engagement with the tensions between different forms of knowledge. At the same time, each professional is challenged to make some attempt to define where they stand in relation to the tensions outlined, and to provide a rationale for this. As the profession grows in confidence we envisage that we can evolve from the 'hesitant hybrid' pointed to by Spinelli (2001a) towards his idea of a field characterized by 'tantalizing innovation'. Our own view is that this is still work in progress but with some very real possibilities. Current trends in the psychological therapies point to an evolving integration where practitioners rarely adhere to single modalities in their work. As Lambert, Bergin and Garfield (2004) point out, a move towards eclecticism and integration 'representing the theoretical joining of two or more positions into a consistent approach, have replaced the dominance of major theories in therapeutic practice' (p. 6). They also point out that the current emphasis on common factors provides an opportunity for less argument in relation to different therapeutic modalities. On the research side, we are also seeing the potential for more integration between research and practice and the rapid expansion of an emphasis on qualitative approaches in the research literature. Our view is that these developments offer both confidence and cohesion to the profession of counselling psychology.

4

PROFESSIONAL TRAINING IN COUNSELLING PSYCHOLOGY

We turn now to the issue of training in counselling psychology, the nature of the programmes that are available, and some recent professional developments in the field. Counselling psychology is now an established profession in a number of countries around the world, with established curricula for postgraduate training. In some other countries certain developments represent work in progress towards such a goal. In the UK we have seen quite a few 'goal post' shifts, especially with the advent recently of the BPS requirement for all accredited programmes to offer a doctoral qualification. In the sections below we firstly consider a global perspective on the nature of training in counselling psychology, with a consideration of the academic-level requirements in particular; and a review of the somewhat unusual 'Independent Route' to training, which is available in the UK. The remaining sections deal with curriculum issues in counselling psychology and the idea of 'the clinical doctorate'; the role of personal therapy as a required part of training; requirements of clinical and research supervision and the nature of, and rationale for, these activities; and the challenges for students in dealing both with theory and with research requirements. We conclude with some comments on the requirement for post training continuing professional development.

Counselling psyhology training: a global perspective

Countries that have a formally recognized counselling psychology profession have related training requirements that fall into one of three categories: a masters level programme, a doctoral level programme, or an independent programme of study. In the sections below we review the situation in different countries and consider the academic and training requirements in more detail. In the appendices we list relevant contact details so that the reader can refer to further relevant information, either to guide a decision to train in this field or to compare counselling psychology training requirements with those in other related helping professions.

In the UK we currently have two options for training towards Chartered Counselling Psychologist status. Applicants may consider either a university-based BPS accredited training programme or the BPS Qualification in Counselling Psychology, generally referred to as the 'Independent Route'. At the time of writing there are nine BPS accredited training programmes in counselling psychology throughout the UK, covering either three years full time, or the equivalent part-time study. Both accredited courses and the independently arranged learning programme need to fulfil the same set of competencies as specified by the BPS Divisions of Counselling Psychology and its related training committees. Overall, the aim is for graduates in counselling psychology to:

1 be competent, reflective, ethically sound, resourceful and informed practitioners of counselling psychology able to work in therapeutic and non-therapeutic contexts;
2 value the imaginative, interpretative, personal and intimate aspects of the practice of counselling psychology;
3 commit themselves to on-going personal and professional development and inquiry;
4 understand, develop and apply models of psychological inquiry for the creation of new knowledge which is appropriate to the multi-dimensional nature of relationships between people;
5 appreciate the significance of wider social, cultural and political domains within which counselling psychology operates; and
6 adopt a questioning and evaluative approach to the philosophy, practice, research and theory which constitutes counselling psychology.

Each of these aims is further subdivided into specific learning outcomes as a guide for courses and trainees (BPS, 2005b). The basic standard for entry into either route of training is the Graduate Basis for Registration (GBR) as specified by the BPS. This is gained via a first degree in psychology, which is recognized by the BPS as conferring GBR status. All potential applicants need to check that their first degree in psychology does actually confer this initial GBR status. Where the GBR status cannot be confirmed it is nevertheless sometimes possible to undertake some additional training modules which, in effect, convert the first degree into the required form. All training and experience undertaken towards chartered status need to post date GBR acquisition, a fact that can be very frustrating for qualified and registered applicants from related helping professions such as psychotherapy who take a degree in psychology after completing their earlier clinical training – in effect those applicants would need to 'start again' in order to achieve chartered status.

In 1994, when the recognition of BPS Chartered Counselling Psychology status was first granted, the BPS offered a 'grandparenting' option to psychologists who had achieved their GBR status but who had subsequently undertaken counselling or psychotherapy training at postgraduate level outside the BPS, and who had also attained relevant postgraduate research skills and experience. Both of us achieved our Chartered Counselling Psychologist status in that way, gaining the BPS Statement of Equivalence to the (as then) Diploma in Counselling Psychology. The decisions concerning what was required to become a counselling psychologist within the UK were influenced by the general requirements for postgraduate training as specified by the BPS, the humanistic base of the counselling professions as a whole, the rejection of the medical model, and an attempt to avoid the 'schoolism' of the various UK professional counselling and psychotherapy organizations. Training needed to cover conceptual knowledge, the development of therapeutic skills through supervised practice with clients, the development of research and evaluation skills appropriate to counselling psychology, and the inclusion of personal development activities covering some experiential work as well as personal therapy. At that time qualification was pitched at masters level, in line with other divisions within the BPS.

Since 2005 the BPS has stipulated that all professionals eligible for chartered status need to have achieved a doctoral level qualification, and all accredited training courses in counselling psychology will now have introduced a doctoral level qualification in place of the previous masters. Training towards chartered status in the UK may also be undertaken by enrolling on the BPS Qualification in Counselling Psychology, commonly referred to as the Independent Route, and not linked directly to the university system. The Qualification is not a course of study; rather, it is a pattern of evidence requirements and assessments around which trainees create their own educational programme. Its origins lie in the BPS Diploma in Counselling Psychology. The BPS more recently renamed this qualification as well as honing its standard towards doctoral (D) level as defined by the Quality Assurance Agency (QAA) for higher education in the UK. This has posed some challenges for the relevant BPS Committees since this route, while granting the Qualification in Counseling Psychology, does not grant the academic title of 'Dr' to its graduates. The move to a doctoral standard of qualification as a chartered counselling psychologist within the UK is also, at present, causing some difficulties with the automatic recognition by the BPS of Irish counselling psychologists already registered with the Psychological Society of Ireland (PSI). The PSI similarly accredits university postgraduate courses in counselling psychology and at present these courses are at masters level. PSI accredited courses require two years' full-time study, or part time equivalent. On completion of formal training and prior to applying for full membership of the Division of Counselling Psychology (DCoP), trainees need to have gained an additional 400 hours of supervised client contact at a ratio of one hour of supervision to eight hours of client contact, with supervision undertaken by a suitably qualified professional (PSI, 2001). However, on-going collaboration is attempting to deal with different anomalies, for example, by allowing European counselling psychologists who are registered with their own professional body, to have their training and practice assessed with a view either to confirming the relevant standard or recommending what additional training and experience might be necessary.

In comparison with other countries, counselling psychology in the USA has been established as a separate specialised training for the longest period of time. The continuing focus on educational- and vocational-based work is often reflected in where the training is based within the university system. For example, a programme might be based in the education department with the award being Doctor of Education upon qualification. To work as a counselling psychologist in both the USA and Canada, professionals need to be granted a licence to practice from the particular state in which they wish to work. To obtain such a licence in any of the states of the USA a doctoral degree in psychology is normally required, although a few states continue to grant licensure at masters degree level. The American Psychological Association (APA) grants specialised accreditation only to doctoral programmes, internships and postdoctoral residency programmes in health service areas of professional psychology which includes counselling psychology.

At present there are approximately 70 accredited counselling psychology programmes in the USA. Training consists of successfully completing a doctoral programme, usually a PhD, but a Psy.D. or Ed.D. are also on offer. These courses consist of four to five years of graduate study involving coursework and integrated training experiences including: instruction in the core areas of psychology such as biological and cognitive/affective areas, as well as the social bases of behaviour; individual differences; history and systems of psychology; specialised instruction in theories of counselling and personality; vocational psychology; human life span development; psychological assessment and evaluation; psychopathology; measurement and statistics, research design; professional ethics, supervision and consultation. Supervised practice focuses on the development of counselling, psychotherapy, assessment and consultation skills. This is followed by the equivalent of a one-year full-time pre-doctoral internship in professional psychology, and the completion of an original psychologically based dissertation. A detailed exploration of training in the USA can be found in Murdock et al. (1998). Once the doctoral training and post-doctoral experience has been completed, one or more further examinations are required before licensure is granted. There is much training in common to both clinical and counselling psychologists in the USA but the main difference continues to be the focus by clinical psychologists on pathology and the medical model, with counselling psychologists focusing on vocational issues and healthy individuals who experience difficulties in living. This reflects philosophical differences in approaches to treatment and research (Leong and Leach, 2007). Counselling psychology in Canada has a sense of being somewhat distinctive from that in the USA but at the same time reflects the connection with North America in terms of training (Young and Nicol, 2007). The Canadian Psychological Association (CPA) accredits doctoral level programmes in a similar way to the APA. The focus in training and practice is upon counselling but from a scientist practitioner standpoint. As mentioned in Chapter 1, there appears to be a divide across the Canadian English–French speaking regions with the French Canadians adopting a similar view to the European French and offering no specific training in counselling psychology in their regions.

In Australia, counselling psychologists are required by law to be registered, with requirements prescribed by individual State and Territory Acts (similar to the arrangements in USA and Canada). While the requirements differ slightly between each State and Territory, the usual requirement is the completion of four full-time years of academic study in psychology, plus an additional period of postgraduate training and supervised experience. Generally, it is necessary to have a masters degree in counselling psychology from an accredited university, plus two years' relevant experience, in order to become a member of the College of Counselling Psychology. In the post-masters degree practice period a supervisor formally assesses the trainee in areas such as: ethical and professional conduct; assessment abilities including the use of psychometric tests; understanding of psychopathology and the formulation of treatment plans; interventions with adults, adolescents, children, couples and families including emphasis on the relationship; and the use and understanding of research to aid in decisions regarding practice. In each geographical area, details of such training require-ments must be obtained from the relevant State and Territory Board. Similarly, New Zealand has statutory registration of psy-chologists and a specialised title of counselling psychologist, and is currently developing coherent training requirements for this spe-cialism in psychology.

In Hong Kong, Korea and China there is considerable blurring of the concept of counsellor, helper and counselling psychologist largely because of the lack of such concepts in the indigenous populations. Reviewing articles within the IAAP special edition of *Applied Psychology: An International Review* (2007) it appears that the strug-gle is indeed to have the 'talking professions' develop within these countries to a professional standard, and to embrace minimal codes of ethics. An additional note of common concern in these countries is the importation of western theories, taught by visiting Westerners. According to Hou and Zhang (2007), we have not as yet seen the development of 'well-constructed, research-confirmed, and cultur-ally accepted indigenous counselling theories' (p. 40). In Hong Kong counselling and counselling psychology are not clearly separated. Clinical and educational psychologists are well established and the Hong Kong Psychological Society's newest Division of Counselling Psychology was formed in 2006. A number of the members of this division were originally trained overseas in USA, Canada and Europe.

In China there are few training courses and those that are offered do not include a practice element in the training. However, progress is taking place with the Chinese Psychological Society forming the Committee of Clinical and Counselling Psychology in 2001. The gov-ernment is aware of the need to build up and regulate the provision of therapy services of all kinds. The Korean Counselling Psychological Association (KCPA), on the other hand, has a certification board which demands a proven level of competence in counselling theory and practice, including clinical supervisor reports, attendance at work-shops, and test administration and interpretation. This is all required at advanced degree level (i.e. postgraduate degree level). Nevertheless, there is no agreed 'core training' at present; suitable clinical placements are hard to obtain and practicum or internships are not yet incorpo-rated into academic postgraduate or doctoral programmes. In Japan the conceptualization and definition of counselling and counselling psychology is still in process. In 2004 the Japanese Association of Counselling Science tentatively proposed such a definition. However, there are as yet no formal counselling or counselling psychology train-ing programmes in Japan although, again, some individuals have trained in other countries such as the USA.

South Africa requires a masters level training as a foundation for statutory registration as a counselling psychologist with the Professional Board for Psychology of the Health Professions Council of South Africa. To practise as a registered counselling psychologist in South Africa trainees are required to complete one year of academic and practical training, a one-year internship at a recognized training site, submit one or more research projects, and sit the national examination set by the Professional Board for Psychology. Clinical, educational and counselling psychologists, following a core training, often study alongside each other and it is the placement, or internship, that defines the different specialties. As previously reviewed in Chapter 1, counselling psychology does not exist as an officially recognized and separate profession in India or Israel, and therefore specialised training is not available. Ensuring that the counselling offered is culturally appropriate is a key issue in the future development of counselling psychology in India:

> The techniques that presently dominate emerge from a western, logical positivist epistemology. These techniques are individualistic in their orientation and to that extent are client-centred and non-directive in their orientation. This may not be effective with clients who come from a collectivistic background. Such a client is 'culturally prepared' to be 'directed'. Learning to deal with this is an example of what could be a key counsellor training issue. (personal communication, G. Arulmani, 2007)

The medical model continues to dominate in Israel with clinical psychologists offering psychological therapies. Most training for those who practice in the mode of counselling psychology is at postgraduate level in counselling, vocational guidance and more recently in coaching.

The International Association of Applied Psychology (IAAP) which was founded in 1920 now has more than 1500 members from more than 80 countries. One of its newest divisions, The Division of Counselling Psychology (Division 16) carries the following statement from the current president, Richard Young:

> As counselling psychology becomes an important area of professional practice and research in an increasing number of countries, it may be helpful if Division 16 can speak to guidelines for the education and training of counselling psychologists. Such guidelines would need to reflect the indigenous understanding and practice of counselling psychology in particular countries and cultures and, at the same time, support local professionals, institutions, and organizations in raising and maintaining standards of effective practice. (http://www.iaapcounselingpsychology.org)

We firmly support these first international moves and hope that they will strengthen the identity and world wide community of counselling psychology. A major issue across different countries and geographical locations in this profession is the focus and awareness of social, cultural and political issues. This awareness of the context within which both clients and professionals live and function is a central characteristic of counselling psychology philosophy and training. Research is also an integral part of counselling psychology training and practice in all settings where the profession is officially regulated. On all established counselling psychology courses, trainees are required to be able to demonstrate an ability to plan, carry out and interpret their own research study and to relate this to practice considerations, and in the USA and UK this ability to demonstrate research competence is, in the majority of trainings, required to be demonstrated at doctoral level. As we highlight below, the integration of research and practice nevertheless remains an on-going challenge in the field, partly as a result of the philosophical and practical demands of positivism within mainstream psychology. However, there are innovative ideas emerging from the counselling psychology and research fields which could pave the way for a better integration between research and practice.

Curriculum issues in counselling psychology

The flexibility and range of knowledge of the original requirements for training in the three major traditions of psychological therapy, as specified originally within the BPS, proved to be popular with many employers as counselling psychologists were able to offer a broad range of therapeutic skills to a wide client population. However, there was also criticism of this breadth of training, with some suggestion that there was not enough specialization in any one particular approach to support a coherent range of skills. Criticism also centred on the capacity of trained professionals to recognize and diagnose serious psychiatric illness and psychopathology. As chartered counselling psychologists began to work in larger numbers within the National Health Service (NHS) the pressure grew to consider these criticisms in more detail. As a member of the small working party in 2004 that considered a revision of the requirements for training in counselling psychology, one of us (Susan) recalls the struggle of balancing what was felt to be the humanistic philosophical base of counselling psychology with the need to ensure that our newly qualified trainees would be able to find employment within organizations such as the NHS, one of the largest employers in the UK. There was a move towards the demands for counselling psychologists to be particularly skilled in their psychotherapeutic knowledge and practice along the lines perhaps of a registered psychotherapist. These moved the training of counselling psychologists more in line with psychologists as psychotherapists in Europe and away from the vocational and educational focus of the USA.

In 2005 the BPS requirements for training in counselling psychology in the UK were revised. The new guidelines specified a range of competencies, requiring a continuing focus on the relationship between therapist and client, but also requiring graduates in counselling psychology to have an in-depth knowledge of one model of psychological therapy and a 'working knowledge' of one other, ideally integrated into a personally meaningful way of working. Additional requirements specified that trainees needed to have a postgraduate level knowledge of theories of change and psychopathology, as well as the ability critically to evaluate these theories; the use and interpretation of tests and other assessment procedures; and an understanding of psychopharmacology as well as the ability critically to evaluate related research and practice. These changes supported the development of a potentially clearer integration within training settings, thus lessening the possibility of 'a little bit of this and a little bit of that' approach. They also supported the development of a more rounded set of skills suitable to contexts such as the NHS. The demand for counselling psychologists to be able to evaluate and carry out research contributing to the knowledge base of counselling psychology has continued as an essential aspect of training. These developments, which in part accommodated requirements from medical settings, reflect a growing trend in many countries where there is considerable competition between counselling and clinical psychologists who both want to access jobs in the national health services.

The recent shift in standard within the UK from masters to doctoral level has also raised a number of interesting challenges within curriculum discussions, and we anticipate that such challenges are also faced by other countries who have needed to make such a change, or who have from the start pondered over the design of a programme which aims both to develop a set of clinical skills as well as meeting the requirements for doctoral level academic work, generally cast within the framework of 'research'. In effect what we now have is the requirement for 'a clinical doctorate' which on the surface might seem non-problematic, but which brings into focus in training settings the tensions between doctoral level academic study and research, and the requirements for the development of clinical skill with clients. All UK accredited training programmes are monitored both by the BPS and by the Quality Assurance Agency for higher education (QAA). In our experience, universities generally engage in more serious monitoring of doctoral level activities than was the case at masters level. One of us (Vanja) has recently developed a previous masters programme into a doctoral level programme for the training of counselling psychologists. One key difference in the requirements is that the doctoral programme needs to be a 'joint programme' with the university in question, thus bringing it directly into a more stringent set of management and assessment rules than was previously the case at masters level, a fact that we understand is generalizable to other universities. Furthermore, the concept of 'doctoral level clinical practice' has yet to be fully understood by the universities, thus potentially perpetuating a lack of integration between research and practice.

Both the BPS and the PSI are organizational members of the European Federation of Psychologists' Associations (EFPA), who have recently drawn up agreed guidelines for the optimal training of all professional psychologists. EFPA is a federation of 32 European national psychological associations, including all of the 25 European Union Member States and seven other European countries, and its member associations represent 165,000 psychologists in Europe. It is an International Non-governmental Organization (INGO) consulting with the European Commission on all matters relating to the standards of education and training, professional practice, and the European recognition of psychologists. A European Certificate in Psychology – the EuroPsy – is currently in development with the intention of offering registration to all eligible psychologists, thus facilitating the free mobility of qualified psychologists throughout Europe. EFPA has agreed on a minimum of six years of training, combining undergraduate and postgraduate studies into the three areas of theoretical knowledge, skills and competencies, and research training (EFPA, 1990). In its July 2006 *Declaration on the European Standards of Education and Training in Professional Psychology*, EFPA has stated that the EuroPsy requirements for qualification for independent practice are completion of education and training in psychology at recognized university level of at least six years' duration, plus a commitment in writing to the ethical code for psychologists in the country of practice and to the European meta-code of ethics for psychologists (see appendices for EFPA contact details). It will be interesting to see how this mutual recognition acts in practice and whether it will extend to what are considered 'specialised trainings' rather than a basic professional accreditation as a psychologist. As outlined in Chapter 1, the Strasbourg Declaration on Psychotherapy (European Association of Psychotherapy, 1990) explicitly defined psychotherapy as a distinct and separate profession from psychology. However, there are professionally accredited and recognized psychologists who are also trained as psychotherapists. It is the emphasis on psychologists practising and specialising in psychotherapy which is also being recognized by EFPA in their current pilot scheme for the Diploma and Advanced Diploma of Psychologists Specialising in Psychotherapy.

The role of personal therapy

The requirement for all counselling psychology trainees to undergo a period of personal therapy was originally highly controversial in the context of other psychological specialties within the BPS. The rationale for this requirement was based partly on the values of counselling psychology, but also on more practical training issues concerned with understanding the experience of therapy from the perspective of a client as well as being able critically and openly to reflect on our own lives and developmental experiences. After much debate, it was decided that 40 hours of personal psychological therapy would be the minimum requirement for all trainees, whether in the context of an accredited programme or the 'independent route'. From the research that we have done, it would seem that the emphasis on personal development of this kind is also a requirement in different countries where counselling psychology is a recognized professional specialty. There is, however, a considerable range in the number of personal therapy hours required in different settings, and on the other forms of personal development that are a part of any training programme. Each course will have its own rationale depending on the type of therapeutic approaches being taught, and on the position that the training team take on the subject of personal development.

Our own view is that practitioners of psychological therapy need to develop a conscious awareness of their own vulnerabilities as well as the development of a high level of resilience. As Hammersley (2003) points out: 'The practitioner will require resilience to survive being exposed to considerable emotional distress, and an attitude of tolerance towards people who are angry, critical or dismissive' (p. 642). O'Brien and Houston (2007) also remind us that research into the effectiveness of therapy highlights the fact that the therapist's self-relatedness 'is positively related to the therapeutic bond, suggesting that the therapist's ability to maintain an open or self-congruent state is beneficial' (p. 76). Legg and Donati (2006) provide a good overview of the values inherent in different forms of both humanistic and psychodynamic therapy where the therapist is not regarded as the person without any 'problems', but as another human being subject to the same distortions and blinkered views as the client. Jung's metaphor of 'the wounded healer' may also be relevant here, highlighting the particular attraction that therapeutic activity may unconsciously hold for the vulnerable person (Hall, 1986; Mander, 2004). Legg and Donati highlight the combination of 'personal sensitivity and emotional toughness' that is likely to be useful in 'the tempestuous voyage of therapy' (2006, p. 222). Personal therapy enables the counselling psychologist to understand their own 'blind spots', thus making it more likely that the client will obtain a better and less 'prejudiced' service. From the point of view of the philosophy and value system of counselling psychology, engagement in personal therapy is part of the commitment to reflexivity and the use of the self, ideas that are relevant both to the practice and the research domains. The centrality of such a value system has been highlighted as key to the on-going learning process in terms of the involvement of both the practitioner and client, or the researcher and researched, in the learning process (Strawbridge and Woolfe, 2003).

Nevertheless, there has also been significant criticism of the requirement for personal development or personal therapy in counselling psychology. Williams and Irving (1996) draw attention to the potentially woolly nature of claims for 'personal development' and the pursuit of 'personal growth', without adequate attention being paid to defining this process in a transparent fashion, and in ways that could lend itself to further focused inquiry. Donati and Watts (2000) take up these ideas, putting forward some useful suggestions for a clearer conceptualization of the personal development process and ways in which this process might be researched in the context of counselling psychology training.

We support the idea of more research that seeks to make some of these complexities more transparent both to trainees and to trainers, and to focus also on the relationship between personal development and selection and assessment processes. One of us (Vanja) has recently initiated a study of the selection process on the course that she manages since the process in that setting involves a consideration of such factors as personal readiness, motivation, and reflective capability at the start of training. Rizq (2005) highlights the frequent emotional struggle that ensues between therapist and client, pointing out also the ways in which such exchanges are often operating at unconscious levels.

Increasingly, research in infant observation (e.g. Schore, 2003b), as well in the complexities of the therapeutic process, require us to conceptualize therapeutic activity as dealing with implicit processes that often may never be made conscious – what Stern (Stern and the Boston Change Process Study Group, 2003) refers to as 'the other side of the moon' (p. 21). The challenges of dealing with early developmental trauma in our work with clients, focusing, for example, on problems of reflective function and mentalization (Fonagy et al., 2004), make it difficult to see how such work can successfully be undertaken without a consideration also of the practitioner's mentalization processes. The considerable demands of the therapeutic process are highlighted also by Rizq (2005) who illuminates the emotional challenges involved in understanding the process of projective identification in client work.

Dealing with theory

Recent curriculum developments in counselling psychology, which have moved the focus away from coverage of the three main approaches to psychological therapy towards a focus only on two approaches, does help to create a somewhat clearer ground for trainees in terms of the literatures that need to be covered. At the same time, we recognize that compared with single modality training there is still an enormous amount of theory to be covered. One of us (Vanja) manages a programme which is based primarily on an integrative framework supported by psychoanalytically informed research and theory and in that setting, trainees need to tackle a very large amount of ideas in the course of their programme of study. It could also be argued that at a doctoral level of training in particular, a candidate would need to have some understanding of the total landscape of possible therapeutic thinking and activity and know how the approaches that they have focused on fit into that landscape. The commitment to pluralism in counselling psychology, and the value base of the profession which stresses contextually based analysis and the reflexive questioning of power processes, is highlighted by Rizq (2006) as potentially very stressful for counselling psychology trainees. She presents a persuasive argument for the emotional relationship that trainees can have with theory, highlighting the student's potential 'emotional difficulty in getting to grips with the dilemma of plurality' (p. 617). From a pluralistic perspective there are no certainties – indeed a commitment to the lack of certainty is a hallmark also of the profession's research attitude – and this can make it difficult for trainees to develop a sense of confidence and psychological authority about their work. At the same time, as highlighted by the UK QAA's descriptors for doctoral level education, a greater 'authoritative' stance is one of the factors which distinguishes doctoral from masters level of study.

The postmodernist turn, which sits well with the conceptual base and practice guidelines of counselling psychology, can also be confusing since in this tradition it often seems that the endless questioning and uncovering of constructed reality can leave the practitioner wondering where to look for some concrete theoretical and practical guidance. Efran and Clarfield (1992), are critical of some of the obscurities of the constructivist approach, suggesting that '[T]herapists adhering to the constructivist perspective often weave a virtually impenetrable fog of abstraction. They talk about creating "multiple conversations simultaneously", bringing about change "unawares", elaborating on the "unsaid", and developing a new connectedness in language' (p. 202). Those authors go on to point out the way that such ideas pose difficulties in imagining an actual therapist working with an actual client. While acknowledging that we are currently in an era of epistemological revolution they go on to suggest that '[C]linicians need to know how constructivism might help them deal more effectively with a quareling couple, a cocaine-addicted teenager, a suicidal husband, a house-bound agoraphobic, an obsessive handwasher, or a high-school dropout' (p. 215). In our chapter on philosophy we also referenced Bekerman and Tatar (2005) who raise the issue of how we might actually meet and deal with a client's distress, suggesting that a postmodern constructivist perspective can be taken too far. Woolfe (2006) presents a developmental view of the profession of counselling psychology, suggesting that the field has now grown into 'a responsible adult' (p. 3). Although this might be a somewhat idealistic view of the human developmental trajectory, we do think that training programmes in counselling psychology need to discuss these dilemmas and challenges openly and collaboratively with trainees, as well as alerting adult learners to such issues at the start of training. As du Plock (2006) suggests, counselling psychology in effect draws its vitality from the capacity to deal with a range of sources, all concerned with what it actually means to be human. The training setting is a part of that process.

Dealing with research

We have earlier referred to the Professional Practice Guidelines for Counselling Psychology (BPS, 2005a) and have highlighted some of the potential tensions that these guidelines bring out in terms of both philosophical issues and approaches to research and its relationship with practice. The scientist-practitioner model, which was originally endorsed for clinical psychology at the Boulder conference in 1949 (Vespia and Sauer, 2006), is also accepted as the guiding template for counselling psychology across many different countries (e.g. Pelling, 2000; Strawbridge and Woolfe, 2003; Lane and Corrie, 2006a). O'Gorman (2001) highlights this model as representing a key philosophy in training courses in the USA, Canada, Australia, New Zealand and the UK. The scientist-practitioner model has nevertheless come under criticism as overly optimistic of what might be possible for professional practice. Some observers argued that while the model was officially accepted it was not followed in practice in many counselling psychology settings (Belar and Perry, 1992).

Some writers, such as Rennie (1994), highlight the existence of a polarity between human science and natural science. McLeod (1999) points out that this distinction is not a new one, preferring instead to conceptualize this as the difference between 'big' research, which deals with large samples, is generally funded and relies on quantification, and 'practitioner' research which is often more locally based with an emphasis on qualitative methods. It was William James who originally expressed the view that the priorities of scientists and practitioners are fundamentally different. We would question this assumption, suggesting instead that the difference in priorities comes from an historical allegiance to different kinds of epistemology. As suggested in our earlier chapter on philosophy, different approaches to epistemology have historically wielded different forms of power, with the dynamics of 'leader' and 'follower' demonstrating a complexity which is not only out of awareness but can be difficult to change. Such dynamics and their implications for organizational functioning have been well documented by writers such as Kets de Vries (1980) and Argyris (2004), and the position of counselling psychology in relation to the 'parent' of mainstream psychology could usefully be analysed in those terms. Many writers have more recently been concerned with the divide of research and practice and the need for more reflection on current paradigms (Goldfried and Wolfe, 1996; Goldfried and Eubanks-Carter, 2004). Hoshmand and Polkinghorne (1992), among others, have taken up this challenge, proposing a revision of the relationship between science and practice in the light of changing postmodern perspectives on epistemology. At the same time, we recognize that the term 'scientist-practitioner' conjures up a number of different perceptions. Corrie and Callanan (2001), for example, conducted an interesting study on the definitions of the scientist-practitioner, concluding that there are a number of different ways that this term may be approached and defined. Lane and Corrie (2006b) seek to reinvent the scientist-practitioner idea, promulgating the view that the concept can evolve in creative ways. However, the roots of the model, in a kind of socially defined positivistic 'rationality', seems to us to underplay the potential artistry of research, and the engagement of the researcher in seeking to throw light on some key questions.

We are more inclined to adopt the idea that research in its most interesting form is a deeply personal issue, what Moran (1999) refers to as the result of 'profound engagement with a quandary, and patient wrestling with it' (p. 45). Viewed in this way, we can discern a much closer connection between what the researcher does and what the therapist and client do together. Moran also alludes to the difficulties that he had in introducing qualitative research methods into a particular counselling psychology training programme, telling us something about the tensions that continue to exist in the field. We might even think about whether the word 'research' is the right one for our field since it tends to be set up as a different activity from 'practice'. We are interested in alternative conceptions such as 'inquiry' (McLeod, 1994; Mair, 1999) since this is a concept that unites research and practice in the therapeutic field. While these issues and debates are interesting in their own right, our focus here is on the implications for professional training in the field of counselling psychology. There is, thankfully, a growing recognition that evidence-based practice and practice-based evidence need to come together in a more coherent way (e.g. McLeod, 2001; Elton Wilson and Barkham, 1994; Barkham and Mellor-Clark, 2003).

These arguments raise issues for the teaching of clinical and research areas within particular counselling psychology trainings. Belar (2000), for example, has suggested that research and practice teaching should not be dealt with separately, arguing for more integration in course design, while Gelso (2006) draws attention to the greater emphasis placed by the majority of training applicants to the practice-based elements of programmes. Of relevance also is the point made by Barrom, Shaddish and Montgomery (1988) that a positive attitude towards research is a good indicator of future research activity among practitioners. We have consistently noticed in our teaching of counselling psychology trainees that we need to engender a renewed enthusiasm for research and its integration with practice, since some of this enthusiasm has frequently been knocked out of individuals through their experiences of first degrees in psychology. Other writers such as Stricker (2002) and Stricker and Trierweiler (2006) draw attention to some of the qualities that characterize research and practice, suggesting the importance of integrating areas that may have significant similarities. Heppner, Wampold and Kivlighan (2008) highlight some of the complexities of research training within the counselling field, suggesting ways that students can be supported in developing an excitement about research activities. If we want our graduates not only to engage in the exploration of research questions but also to influence the world of service delivery and the quality of what is offered to potential clients, then we need to address both the issues of real-world research (Robson, 2002) and engage with those approaches, such as action research, that are concerned both with the production of knowledge and with useful social change (e.g. Reason and Bradbury, 2008).

The supervision of practice and research

Trainees in counselling psychology will be offered supervision for both their clinical work with clients and the development of their research projects. The supervision of clinical work is a requirement, both during training and after qualification, and is a part of the ethical frameworks for practice for all counselling and psychotherapeutic professional bodies. Different professional bodies have different requirements for the amount and frequency of clinical supervision, and there may also be differences in course requirements depending on how this activity is viewed by a specific course team. For example, in the training setting, supervision is a space for the review of work with clients as well as a place where trainees can discuss the overall development of their learning on the course in question, and the amount of supervision required might need to be balanced across those different types of conversations. Also, as we have seen in relation to some programmes in other countries, the clinical supervisor can function in addition as an important assessor, ahead of formal registration. Indeed, training supervisors are generally assessors of some kind since they will need to complete a supervisor's report for each individual trainee, usually on an annual basis. This raises the issue of dual roles in supervision and points to some of the potential dilemmas, difficulties and challenges which can arise both for supervisors and for supervisees (see Lawton and Feltham, 2000). Different definitions of supervision, and an illumination of the tasks and functions of this activity, have been outlined by a range of writers (e.g. Holloway, 1995; Carroll, 1996; Hawkins and Shohet, 2000; Gilbert and Evans, 2000; Orlans and Edwards, 2001a). Overall, clinical supervision offers a range of opportunities for trainees. It is a learning setting, concerned both with personal and professional matters since, in our view, those areas are not possible to separate when dealing with relational matters; it is an opportunity for support; it comprises a setting for the quality checking of the service offered to clients; and it functions as a demonstration of a commitment to ethical and practice requirements. As McCann (2006) points out, in training settings there are usually three distinct systems involved in the supervision process, the training institute, the supervisor and the trainee, and the placement setting. Generally, some supervision will take place in the training setting, and some in the placement setting, and may be conducted on a one-to-one or group basis.

Very little attention has been paid, in our view, to the subject of research supervision. While research supervision is not an ethical requirement and therefore differs in that regard from clinical supervision it is no less important in the training context and also brings with it a number of complexities. In the past, research supervision has, in the context, for example, of the UK PhD system, been generally a somewhat unorganized activity. Some universities are quite good at recognizing the need for a regular exchange of ideas and updates on progress, either in individual or group contexts, while others take a more laissez faire attitude. Our own commitment is to a practitioner research philosophy, which involves both doctoral level activity and the development of an authoritative stance which comes through in the work itself as well as in its oral presentation. This kind of work is much more process based, involving the whole person of the researcher, as well as the relationship between researcher and researched, and supervisor and supervisee. It is not just a matter of the content of the research, but also has to do with the developing self of the researcher so that the level of authority required at doctoral level can be adequately conveyed, both in writing and in person. This kind of supervision requires the supervisor firstly to recognize and understand some of the complexities involved, and secondly to be willing and to have the skill to spot the difference between the need for intellectual or practical support and the need for emotional and developmental support. Very little attention has been paid in the literature to an analysis of this kind of academic supervision. A notable exception is provided by Barbara Grant (Grant, 1999) who outlines some of the complexities in the supervision of graduate students, arguing for a more integrated perspective on this activity, with the importance also of attending to the multiple relationship factors which may be discerned in this process.

Continuing professional development

We conclude this chapter with a few comments on the role of continuing professional development (CPD). CPD became mandatory in the BPS in 2000 for all Chartered Psychologists holding a Practising Certificate. Practitioners are required to record and submit at least 40 hours of CPD activity per year and are encouraged both to plan each year of activities in advance and to record reflections on learning outcomes. The underlying philosophy is concerned with the principle of on-going learning and development as a way of keeping fresh in our work, as well as keeping abreast of developments in professional thinking and practice. While this can be viewed as yet another bureaucratic requirement, we support this development in the field as it serves to challenge professionals to think about on-going development beyond the training setting, and to consider how they can develop and retain a liveliness in a professional field that is often challenging and which can lead, in the worst case, to burnout. As we are currently in the process of entering the domain of statutory regulation we shall have to see what effect this is likely to have on the monitoring of continuing professional development. We understand that CPD activities are likely in time to be monitored by the Health Professions Council (HPC) and at the time of writing we do not know how this might change the current emphasis.

5

CAREERS AND PRACTICE IN COUNSELLING PSYCHOLOGY

In terms of practice settings, trainees of accredited programmes are encouraged to develop skills and experience in a number of different contexts and modalities. This is highlighted, for example, in the BPS guidelines for accreditation of courses (BPS, 2006) which state that trainees need to provide services in different settings and 'operate safely and professionally in a range of modalities, contexts and time-frames of therapeutic practice' (p. 10). Modalities are defined as work with individuals, couples, groups, families and organizations. In relation to BPS-accredited training programmes in the UK, we can discern a wide range of philosophical positions, as well as the offer of different combinations of therapeutic approaches. In practice, trainees in the UK, as well as in other countries, realize that they need to make choices as all contexts or approaches cannot be covered. Trainees on the independent route in the UK also need to make decisions of this kind, and are subject to the same regulatory framework as applies to course routes. The potential range of possibilities presents both opportunities and limitations. On the plus side, individuals can plan their own specialist pathway from a career point of view, with many options available over time. The downside is that it makes it more difficult for the profession to have a clearly boundaried identity for the benefit especially of potential employers and clients. However, all qualified Chartered Counselling Psychologists are required, on successful completion of their chosen training path, to have demonstrated the agreed BPS competencies for this professional field (see appendices) which reflect a generic set of learning outcomes. We consider that the development of these competencies provides a coherent skill base which can be applied in a number of different contexts. We shall return to considerations of identity in our final chapter.

In the sections below we provide an overview of some of the different settings in which counselling psychologists might work. Settings covered include national mental health services, secure environments and forensic settings, the legal setting, the organizational context, independent practice and academia. We also include a short narrative on the experience of undertaking training in more than one country, a situation which is not uncommon, and which could potentially increase with the support of organizations like the European Federation of Psychologists' Associations (EFPA). Overall, there is a mix of the different modalities referred to earlier. In order to bring particular professional settings alive we have included a short narrative constructed from reports of individuals working in these different settings. Where appropriate, names and any identifying characteristics have been changed. We conclude with some reflections on employment issues in the field, with particular reference to the UK situation.

National Mental Health Services

The majority of counselling psychologists in the UK are now employed within the National Health Service (NHS) in a variety of posts. During the early years of professional development in the UK, counselling psychologists were most commonly employed within primary care, working either as part of a primary care team (a team of professionals working with a general practitioner) or as part of a hospital psychology service with outreach services to GP surgeries. Counselling psychologists were employed as skilled therapists to work with clients who did not necessarily need the input of a psychiatrist or hospital-based care. Jane's description below shows how far this involvement at primary care level has developed within many areas, highlighting the multifaceted nature of her current role:

When I came into post in this NHS trust, my brief was to develop and run the rural primary care service in conjunction with my colleagues in the city primary care service. I have been the psychologist in the rural service since its inception and when I started, I had one psychology assistant and a list of GP surgeries that might consider giving me space to work. From these rather limited beginnings, the primary care service now holds clinics in seven GP surgeries and takes referrals from all the rural GPs, psychiatry, the psychological treatment service and the community mental health team. There is no self-referral, but patients can ask their GP to refer them for an assessment if they wish. We have also developed a 'books on prescription' service, which is a list of self-help books that are recommended by the service and can either be bought or borrowed, free of charge, from any local city library. The client does not need to be a member of any library; they can access the book with a prescription from their GP. Part of my role is to write self-help manuals when needed, develop the service, and offer supervision and training to the psychology assistant and the counsellor's supervisor. I also sit on the committee that is responsible for developing the role of primary care across the whole of the region. My therapy work in primary care consists of doing all the assessments for the rural service and some of the more complex CBT work. All referrals are sent directly to me. Those whom I think are not suitable for primary care I either refer on to secondary care at the psychological treatment service, or psychiatry and the community mental health team. I also work in secondary care one day a week doing assessments and cognitive behaviour therapy and offer training to nurses and GPs on mental health issues in primary care settings. The mental health service is about to undergo a radical revision in the next few months and the emphasis is going to be on developing services in primary care and away from hospital settings. We will be gaining the services of a gateway worker and possibly a community psychiatric nurse in primary care, as well as incorporating a stepped care approach. As the psychologist, I expect the managerial part of my role to expand, although I will still keep my day in secondary care as well as some client work in primary care. Being trained as a counsellor rather than as a clinical psychologist has helped enormously in working in this kind of setting. It is vital to be able to understand both clients and GPs in a holistic way, to represent both across the mental health service, and to be able to separate out and take account of different narratives and perspectives so that the whole system runs smoothly. In this area counselling psychology has parity with clinical psychology.

This description demonstrates the very broad range of responsibilities that a counselling psychologist might have within the NHS setting, as well as the need to take an authoritative stance and be prepared to contribute to on-going developments such as, for example, the community-oriented primary care approach (Lenihan and Iliffe, 2000), or the current triage system where a number of different gateways exist for client referral (see Smallwood, 2002, for a personal perspective). One account in the literature (Sugg, 2007) demonstrates the way that counselling psychologists can feel at home in the medical environment of the NHS, both respecting and working with the medical model while not losing their own identity and humanistic standpoint.

Counselling psychologists are now employed throughout the mental health services of the NHS, in secondary (specialised) and tertiary (highly specialised) care, working with a range of clients and offering a variety of services. The Child and Adolescent Mental Health Service (CAMHS) for example, provides a range of opportunities for counselling psychologists to become involved in interdisciplinary teams concerned with the mental health of young people, including those with learning disabilities (e.g. Georgopoulou, 2007). Below is a description of some of Margaret's duties in such a setting while she was still training. Here we see the challenge of the range of professional knowledge that is often required in this field, and the way in which this might not always be available within the particular training path that the individual has chosen:

Working with children and young people necessitated the development of a whole new range of communication skills, interventions and techniques in order to develop rapport, identify the factors contributing to presenting difficulties, build the therapeutic relationship, and implement successful interventions such as drawing, story telling, discussion of pictures, play therapy, guided fantasy, and behavioural interventions. It was the first time that I had used supervision almost as a 'master-class' in technique. It was only through the skill and support of a highly competent and experienced supervisor, and a willingness to undertake what amounted to an extra module's worth of independent study, that I was able to practise competently and ethically in this area, without the support of a taught module at the university. Although the primary focus of the work was the child, it was both impossible and inappropriate to ignore their families and other social systems of which they were a part. This necessitated working from a systems perspective (Bowen, 1985) in order to explore and understand the unhelpful behaviour patterns that may have been operating in, or absorbed from, the family (or wider) system and work towards change. Therapy would typically involve individual work with the child, group work with the family as a whole and often work with the parents to address concerns and work on parenting skills. In some cases, I also offered one-to-one therapy to work on an individual parent's issues which required a very high level of flexibility and the careful management of confidentiality issues. Interaction with, and consultation to, educational services was another important part of my Child and Family work, which included behavioural monitoring in the school setting; interviewing and providing information to teachers and support workers; and liaising with child psychiatrists, educational psychologists, school nurses, and third party organizations like Autism Outreach. I produced behavioural monitoring material for use both at home and in school, presented on behalf of the Child and Family service at Statement Review Meetings, and attended review meetings in school with the child and parents. I also held meetings with both the Head of the Home and Hospital Tuition Service and Home Tutors to discuss and advise upon clients' progress, and develop re-integration strategies for return to main-stream education.

The highest level of employment within the NHS is as a consultant counselling psychologist. In some areas of the UK consultant counselling psychologists are also becoming heads of psychology departments, making decisions on psychological provision, as well as managing budgets. Walsh (2007) describes the multifaceted nature of this role and the way that she has to move between many different functions covering clinical, managerial and leadership functions. Below is a further account from John, another consultant counselling psychologist which also highlights the diverse nature of this role:

There is no typical working day or week in my role as a Consultant Counselling Psychologist and Psychology Service Manager in an NHS Trust Adult Mental Health service. That is both the challenge and the attraction of the role. What follows is based on my diary for the past week which is not necessarily typical. I started the week off on Monday with some self-nourishment by attending a CPD event on mindfulness-based CBT. It's rare that I allow myself the time to do things like this, so it was a bit of a treat. It also turned out to be an opportunity to catch up with some colleagues from other areas of the country who sit on the same committees as I do, and some of the lunch break and a period at the end of the day were spent in discussion about national NHS psychology workforce issues and our attempts to meet with civil servants and ministers to discuss these. Tuesday began with an early morning meeting of my Trust's Psychological Therapies Committee working party tasked with mapping demand and supply of psychological therapies in the Trust area. This was immediately followed by a meeting of a group developing an integrated care pathway for clients with borderline personality disorder. Both of these meetings were multiprofessional and presented a

(Continued)

challenge in encouraging people to subsume personal and professional agendas for the common good. I feel optimistic that we are making progress on this. After a quick lunch I am off to one of our outlying Community Mental Health Teams, where I am scheduled to provide supervision for the team and then see two clients. Generally my role these days as far as direct client work is concerned is to see people that colleagues have found challenging. Wednesday saw me in my office for the first time this week, and I had an hour to catch up with my secretary, the mail and emails, before I chaired a meeting of EMDR practitioners from my own and neighbouring Trusts. Then it was off to the Department of Psychological Medicine in the District General Hospital where I provide clinical supervision to the staff of psychologists, counsellors and psychotherapists. In the evening I intended to get down to writing a long-planned paper on the influence of certain early psychoanalysts on the development of counselling psychology, but was yet again distracted, this time by the football on TV. On Thursday I chaired the regular bi-monthly meeting of my psychology service. We employ clinical and counselling psychologists, counsellors and therapists, and deliver services in primary and secondary mental health care, physical health, and staff counselling, so there is always plenty to discuss. This morning I updated the team on proposed national and local changes in service structures, and then a colleague fed back to us on a training event she had recently been to on CBT for psychosis. After this I gave supervision to one of my team who provides a counselling service at our neighbouring hospital. On Friday I was meant to be attending a meeting on implementing the NHS Knowledge and Skills Framework in the Trust, but this was postponed so I was able to get to my desk and tackle some of the waiting jobs. These included reviewing the job description for one of the posts in the service, writing up a proposal for funding for a pilot psycho-educational group programme, trying to make sense of my service budget to see if we can offer a paid post for a counselling psychology trainee, and checking some costings supplied by the finance department for our contract to provide staff counselling to another Trust. Not a typical week but then no such thing exists – but certainly another week full of both interest and headaches.

One of the major challenges of working within the NHS is that of working within a state structure that is based upon the medical model of diagnosis and the planning of subsequent treatments to effect a cure. Counselling psychologists in those settings work as part of a team, alongside clinical psychologists and psychiatrists, with clients who have been diagnosed as mentally ill. While the evidence-based clinical interventions of the counselling psychologists might look rather similar to those of their colleagues, their thinking about the problems and their desire to form a relationship with the client is likely to be markedly different. However, most counselling psychologists are open to finding a way to work in multidisciplinary settings, notwithstanding some of the complexities involved (e.g. Corney, 2003). There are certainly challenges in this setting but, as we have seen from the accounts above, there are also many interesting activities and satisfactions to be enjoyed.

Secure environments and forensic settings

The most difficult challenge for counselling psychologists working within prison and forensic settings is to maintain a philosophical stance independent of that which is both implicit and explicit in such settings. There is an obvious parallel with those counselling psychologists who work within the NHS of maintaining a stance independent of the medical model. In prison settings, the organization as a whole is focused upon the protection of the public and in maintaining 'law and order'. There can be some ambivalence towards 'prisoners', depending on the nature of the crime as well as the state of mind of the prisoner. In some high secure settings, the work can potentially be dangerous so there is the challenge both of taking in the reality of that position while holding on to a set of humanistic values, and treating the client holistically rather than reducing the person to their 'crime'. Research has shown that early environmental deficits, attachment disorders and problems of addiction are a part of the backgrounds of many people who pursue a criminal career and that prison populations have a particularly high risk of suicide (Towl and Crighton, 2002). This points to the importance of psychological and therapeutic resources being a part of any prison setting. Professionals in those settings may also be dealing with cognitive and neurological impairment which has precipitated criminal activity. The potential for suicide, and its actual occurrence, has implications for all staff in those settings. A recent study of prison officers who had experienced a death in custody demonstrated the need also for the psychological support of those members of staff (Wright et al., 2006).

While settings vary, inmates are often treated as well as possible in difficult circumstances. However, the nature of the culture in such settings tends towards the impersonal, with control reflected in both the endless security focus and the language between professionals. Prison-based jargon is prevalent, reducing interpersonal exchanges of information to numbers, sections and acronyms, thus highlighting the impersonal and structural. There is also a different approach to confidentiality, although this, to some extent, also parallels health service settings and multidisciplinary work. Clients in secure environments are often required to attend therapy, with this being linked to the possibility of parole. This makes it difficult to proceed with open contracting and shared dialogue of the kind that is usually emphasized in the context of therapeutic training. The following short narrative from Mark brings out the particular challenges of working in this setting:

I have had a number of different jobs as a counselling psychologist in secure settings over the last ten years. I find the work both fascinating and difficult at times. I am aware on the one hand that my clients are in this secure environment as the result of committing a crime. At the same time I am familiar with research which points to the deprived backgrounds of prisoners, research that is also supported by my experience of this work. All my clients have been men. The majority of my clients are required to attend counselling and are aware that a refusal to do so will affect their chances of parole. Often, they have had little experience of being treated with humanity, either in their early experiences, in their peer groups or in the prison setting. It is also not unusual for these men to have had many prison experiences. On release they often return to the same peer group and lifestyle since no other is available to them. Achieving any kind of working alliance can be difficult under these circumstances. Also, the regularity of our sessions can be cut across by the prisoner being transferred to another prison without notice, or occasionally the prison going into 'lock down' status, preventing either of us making our session. So what keeps me interested in this work you might ask? There is something about these outwardly macho men, often violent, often bright and manipulative, but also often humorous and contactful once they believe that I am more or less trustworthy, that has impacted me; something about the deep humanity that can remain present whatever the circumstances. The nature of these men's stories also get to me – fathers who were murdered before their eyes, violent beatings when very young, sexual abuse and environments with zero trust and limited resources. Depression and suicidal feelings are not uncommon and there are policies about how to deal with these, which include open communication with other staff which places limits on the level of confidentiality that I can maintain. I am grateful for the quality of supervision that I have consistently received which has, I think, enabled me to avoid the potential for burnout that can come from listening to accounts of traumatic experiences and knowing often that my input will not lead to life-changing outcomes. I am also grateful to my own personal therapy which has enabled me to understand the support that I need to access in this work, ensuring also that I do not become over identified with my clients. Arriving at work for my sessions was strange at the beginning although now I am used to it. A typical procedure has been as follows: a large gate is opened following the checking of my identity. I am then led through a series of locked doors – there is the sound of keys and metal clanking as we go into yet another corridor. Finally we come to my 'consulting room', a room which has a panel in the door that can be opened, and where there is an alarm by my chair. At least one prison officer sits outside this room while I run my sessions. Any unexpected noise can result in the panel in the door being opened and a voice saying 'alright?'; the activating of the alarm will see several armed officers enter the room. Luckily I have not had many experiences of the latter. I have come to understand some of the necessity for these procedures and it doesn't really get to me any more, but I can't help feeling that we are all caught up in a strange culture. Occasionally my clients and I talk about the situation and I think about Goffman's work (Goffman, 1968) and what he would make of my setting. I am working towards better facilities for my sessions and more flexibility however, since my formulations concerning which clients are likely to be unsafe are generally correct. I work in a multidisciplinary team which includes psychiatrists and forensic psychologists. Team morale is exceptionally good, and I sometimes wonder about the way that this might be supported by an underlying sense of fear that pervades the prison culture.

Counselling psychologists are employed in increasing numbers within secure settings to work alongside their forensic psychology colleagues. Counselling psychologists offer assessment and formulation skills and the ability to offer prisoners various forms of therapeutic input, from brief counselling to specialised therapeutic activities and group work. The greatest challenge is to bring the focus of contact with their client back to the relationship between client and therapist. The work offers the opportunity both of some structured activity which can help in the management of life in prison as well as preparation for the outside world, and the possibility of offering a relational framework and experience to a person whose history is unlikely to include such contact. As we saw in the above vignette, there are particular factors in this setting which make this a challenging task.

The legal setting

The court system makes use of counselling psychologists to produce reports for consideration both at hearings and also, where appropriate, to advise a judge regarding sentencing. The focus of the report will depend upon the court setting, i.e. criminal court, civil court or family court, as well as the instructions of the commissioning solicitor. The counselling psychologist is usually expected to assess and provide a formulation on the person or persons interviewed and to make recommendations to the court regarding therapeutic treatment and the indication of any perceived future risks, both to the person interviewed and their possible risk to others. A fully trained counselling psychologist is seen as a blend of 'scientist-practitioner' and reflexive therapist able to present a full picture of an individual or family to the court. The ability to blend the use of standardised psychometric tests and formulation is seen as useful to the courts and informative to the different parties involved. Emma's account below provides a good overview of work in this setting:

I practise in two main areas of the legal system in the UK: the family courts and the criminal courts. Most of my work is funded by the legal aid system where the individuals concerned would not otherwise be able to engage either legal or other 'expert' representation. I have a background in systemic family therapy and am often involved in cases concerning children being taken into care. My instructions may come from one particular person's solicitor but in the family courts the intention is always to act in the best interests of the children so the instructions are agreed between all parties involved. As the counselling psychologist expert witness, it is my job to prepare a report to aid the court in any decisions it makes about the children. It is important not to make decisions about what is happening within the family or focus on 'blame' but rather to consider what the known facts are, to use psychological skills to understand further what might be happening considering the therapeutic and research knowledge currently available and then to come to some conclusions. I find that this work is rather similar to preparing a client case study where one needs to tie one's understanding of what has happened to a particular model of therapy and to research papers to arrive at a 'differential diagnosis' saying that this needs to be considered but it also might be influenced by this or this. I liaise with many agencies as well as professionals such as psychiatrists, probation officers, social workers and solicitors. Although in theory the psychological report in the criminal courts is also intended to be unbiased there is a great deal of pressure to write a report which supports the side who instructed you (defence or prosecution). The work with clients in the criminal setting is the single client study carried out in detail so it often includes life history, ability and personality assessment, present emotional and psychiatric state. The main liaison is most frequently with other psychologists or psychiatrists and solicitors. There is frequently a long time delay between preparing a report and appearing in a court hearing. I find it important to remember that I am not on any 'side' during these hearings but am there as an expert witness to inform the court with an independent psychologist's opinion which I interpret as similar to providing psycho-education. I try to find a way to articulate what needs to be said in a language that is not full of psychological jargon and to be prepared to explain further when it is clear a barrister or judge has not fully grasped certain points. Sometimes I spend the whole day waiting to appear only to be told that I am no longer needed because of some point of law or because the 'other' side accepts the report in full and no longer plans to question its recommendations. Doing this work brings me into contact with what can sometimes feel like a strange world of lawyers and courtrooms where decisions are made that will often have a profound effect on an individual or family life. It is stressful, especially if you are not at all sure about what is going on in someone's life so do not have the 'firm' opinion the legal system likes so much. I cope by seeing the court system as the one that decides on other people's futures and remind myself that I am simply there to inform.

Court work of various kinds is now recognized as a key activity of psychologists across different divisions of the BPS. This work is quite specialised and is supported by the BPS through the publication of various relevant reports, for example, to do with child and family work (The Law Society, 2006; BPS, 2007b), to do with the role of the expert witness (BPS, 2007c), and a review of the use of psychometric tests in the court setting (BPS, 2007d).

Organizational contexts

There are a number of key contributions that counselling psychology can make to the work setting (Orlans, 2003), and there are challenges as well as excitements in adapting a more clinical perspective to that context (Orlans and Edwards, 2001b). The presence of 'the organization' as a continuous third party, and a prevailing value system that can prioritize 'bottom line' financial efficiencies over humanistic concerns, can pose dilemmas for counselling psychologists, an issue explored also by Kinder (2007). Nevertheless, counselling at work has been a growing field over recent years, offering many opportunities for graduates in the counselling psychology profession to utilize both their clinical and research skills. Evaluation of counselling services within the work setting offers an obvious opportunity potentially to bring together research and service development (Alker and Cooper, 2007; Elliott and Williams, 2002). There are a number of different job roles that a counselling psychologist can take on in relation to organizational settings. One possibility is a full-time post within, for example, the human resources department, functioning in part as an internal consultant, running training days, liaising with teams on developmental issues and seeing some clients on an individual basis, generally for short-term work. Large organizations, such as the Post Office, have for a long time had a counselling service in place in order to provide staff with support on issues which may affect their ability to carry out their jobs (Tehrani, 1995, 1997). This type of system functions as an internal Employee Assistance Programme (EAP), although that facility can also be on offer from an external provider. EAPs have increased in popularity over recent years and are now fairly commonplace in large organizations. Generally, counsellors or counselling psychologists will be employed as 'affiliates' which means that they are, in effect, self-employed but sign an agreement to adopt the protocol of the organization in relation to clients that they see. This means agreeing to certain confidentiality issues; for example, if there is a suicide risk it may be required to report this to management. This also involves the counselling psychologist in a three-way contract between client, therapist and organization, and in an agreement to complete relevant paperwork for each case. There are management-level responsibilities involved in such roles, particularly for counselling psychologists who have research experience. This is evidenced by the following short narrative by Ray:

I am employed by a healthcare provider Employee Assistance Programme as a Clinical Governance and Training Manager. My EAP work involves clinical audit, supervision, clinical training, and writing clinical protocols and guidelines in line with relevant research. I am responsible for monitoring the quality of the round-the-clock counselling service provided to employees of 'client' companies and therefore investigate and monitor all complaints of a clinical nature, which can involve the in-house service or face-to-face counselling with a member of our large nationwide affiliate network of psychologists and counsellors. It is my responsibility to keep up to date with professional issues such as statutory regulation, and to feed back at departmental level and at a company level as a member of the multidisciplinary Clinical Governance Board. I organize an annual conference for our team of counsellors and psychologists and manage the department's training budget to support our staff with their continuing professional development. I also provide overnight psychologist on-call cover to support the counselling team in cases of clinical emergency or complexity.

It is not uncommon for individuals to come into counselling psychology from another career. Sometimes a personal crisis brings 'counselling' into the frame and the person begins to follow a different way of viewing the world. Sometimes certain professional activities overlap which we find now to be the case with counselling and coaching (Orlans, 2008). In the vignette below, Ginny outlines her experiences in investment banking, indicating the varied backgrounds that a counselling psychologist might have, and highlighting also the overlapping nature of the domains of coaching and counselling:

The coaching work I do is informed by my previous 23 years' experience of working for a major US investment bank and a firm of city consultants. To give you an overview of my 'pre-psychologist' career: I did some of my banking exams in my early 20s and worked in the banking business. I worked for a very senior investment banker, with money market traders and finance directors, learning how to market, sell, put proposals together etc. I trained on the job to design and run courses, was sent off to our head office in New York to learn how to deliver various courses, and to college in the UK where I completed being a training officer. In the middle of all of this I did a psychology degree at night school. I continued to offer a range of training courses to the mixed community of individuals found in investment banks – investment bankers, traders, lawyers, accountants, IT staff and clerical staff through to maintenance, messengers, architects, plumbers, chauffeurs, and chefs. I also trained clients who would come to the UK for training from large banks throughout the world. The types of courses I ran included courses on leadership and communication and I delivered these in Europe

(Continued)

for staff from European offices. This work gave me invaluable experience in one-to-one coaching with very diverse cross-cultural groups of people. I gained further insight into business requirements and different roles during a period when I recruited staff for about three years, and subsequently through working for a consultancy where I designed and delivered management development courses both in the UK and abroad. During my counselling psychology training I freelanced and got into out placement in the City on the back of my knowledge and experience with investment banks. This led to an interest in career coaching which in turn led me to undertake further training in occupational psychology. Unfortunately, this latter training really taught me nothing new given my previous experience. Most of my current work involves counselling – the whole range covering anxiety, anger, depression, self-esteem, relationships, losses and adjustments, child abuse, and quite a lot of trauma. I also conduct assessments, and over the last 18 months have become involved in writing legal reports. I have been self-employed since about 1996 and built this practice up by initially doing a part-time role as a trainer and gradually moving to total self-employed status about seven years ago. I now see between 20–25 people a week.

It is not unusual in our experience for counselling psychologists to have varied backgrounds of this kind, with counselling psychology representing a second career. One of us (Vanja) manages an accredited counselling psychology training programme where there is an explicit requirement for applicants to have work-based experiences. In practice these experiences are rich and varied, with individuals bringing a wide range of existing skills into their new profession. The other issue highlighted by Ginny's account above is the self-employed status of many counselling psychology graduates who often have a number of different job roles as well as a clinical practice. We review that position in more detail below.

Independent practice

Many counselling psychology graduates undertake a range of job roles, perhaps with a part-time position in an NHS setting, supplemented by some teaching and the maintaining of a private practice. Alan Frankland (2007) explores the notion of the counselling psychologist as a 'portfolio professional' developing an idea from

Charles Handy (1989) of an expanding group of workers who do not take on a traditional path of employee within only one organizational setting. Alan says:

> I identify seven different kinds of activity or strands that appear within my portfolio as a counselling psychologist; in any one week any one of them may be dominant (or not appear at all), and in any one day I might do some work in almost every category. At present (and in descending order of involvement as shown by averaging hours over the last six weeks) my portfolio is made up of the following .... (p. 42)

Alan goes on to outline the different activities in his portfolio which are as follows: a supervision practice with 18 supervisees from a range of settings and with different needs; short-term and long-term therapeutic work both of approximately eight hours a week; work in the NHS through a consultant post dealing with a range of tasks including policy matters regarding dual diagnosis, skill development, and training; professional administration of his own practice and the NHS work; training commitments; writing a book; and what he describes as 'miscellaneous professional time' covering continuing professional development (CPD), reading and research. He paints a picture of a varied set of activities, each bringing its own satisfactions and challenges. Joan Staples, writing in the same issue of *Counselling Psychology Review* (Staples, 2007), presents a vivid picture of the counselling psychologist in private practice, a picture which suggests independence, breathing space, creative potential, as well as some risk. Joan describes a long history as both an occupational and counselling psychologist, and the way that she worked herself towards a private practice 'over the space of 10 years and two children' (p. 35). She goes on to say:

> In my view being alone in private practice helps if you have the personality suited to risk taking and working to the limits of your confidence. It may be that some of you will set up with a given population and already prescribed specialism(s) with which you are most familiar. That is an excellent start. For me the stepping stone took the form of the part time 'day job' underpinning my counselling practice. For you it could be a part-time contract like clinical sessions or visiting lecturer/tutor at the local university/college. (p. 36)

Joan goes on to offer a number of guidelines to anyone interested in taking the private practice route in their career. Her guidelines include design factors, professional considerations, financial matters, and psychological issues. There is obviously an overlap between the focus on private clinical practice, that is, the provision of therapy and supervision, and the portfolio approach outlined earlier which includes both a private clinical practice and some other professional activities.

Academic settings

Qualified counselling psychologists who have developed consider-able skill and experience in the therapeutic setting, as well as per-haps pursuing research projects and other managerial activities, are often well suited to an academic setting. This is especially true now that chartered counselling psychologists are required by the BPS to be working at doctoral level. Many people who invest the time and effort to pursue doctoral level studies, particularly in a university setting, develop an affinity with the academic values that they work within and are well placed to take up positions as lecturers, senior lecturers or principal lecturers, depending on their level of academic experience. Katrina Alilovic (2007) describes her entry into a full-time lecturer appointment, and the challenge of the requirement of combining the roles of teacher, researcher and practitioner in that setting. She brings out the way in which a counselling psychologist perspective offers the opportunity to retain a holistic approach to the integration of these different roles:

> Counselling practice underpins all that I do in my role as a lecturer. ... The experiences and knowledge I've accumulated are helpful to me in creating and facilitating learning opportunities. These opportunities will hopefully support trainees in developing their understanding of themselves in relation to how best to support their clients. The pri-vate work extends the overall time I spend working and it's a chal-lenge to fit it all in and maintain some sense of balance and well-being. I occasionally succeed. However, I believe it is an impera-tive to keep as close as I can to the heart of what I'm teaching. No 'ivory tower' here. (p. 6)

Katrina's account highlights both some of the tensions in this arrangement as well as some of the benefits both to her and to the trainees. One of us (Vanja) is deeply involved in academia and has this to say about that form of professional life:

> I manage a BPS accredited doctoral programme for the training of counselling psychologists. While this has posed some challenges over the last couple of years with the shift from masters to doctoral level, I have also been very interested in the standards prescribed by the Quality Assurance Agency (QAA) in the UK for higher educa-tion and the challenge of adapting these to the development of pro-fessionals who are learning how to integrate theory, research and clinical practice at doctoral level. Although I am often stressed by the

changing professional goal posts, the bureaucratic nature of higher education, and the endless external requirements for professional advancement and accreditation, I love the opportunity of working in an environment where I can play with ideas and philosophies, think about the complexities of learning and teaching, and talk with my students about the challenge of bringing humanistic ideas together with academic requirements. The work involves a wide variety of management responsibilities, team work, liaising with many different professionals in a range of settings, attending to programme design and curriculum development, keeping abreast of teaching materials, managing research projects, interacting with trainees and staff, and doing things like writing student handbooks, reports and references as well as academic articles. There are times when everything feels too busy – especially when my 'to do' list goes beyond one side of A4 and things begin to drop off the end of it! However, I particularly enjoy creating and supporting good learning environments, the details of programme development, the exchanges with candidates, and the feeling that I have made some difference in the trajectory of a person's life, as well as having made a contribution to the broader field through a candidate's impact on their professional and personal worlds.

Academic responsibilities can be combined with other professional activities. As highlighted earlier in our section on independent practice, there are many counselling psychologists who have a part-time academic appointment as well as responsibilities which include a private practice. It is difficult to ascertain the mood of the profession at this time but there does seem to be significant interest in not being in total allegiance to just one 'employer'.

International integration

We have referred in an earlier chapter to the fact that a number of our colleagues around the globe have come to either the USA or the UK to train as a counselling psychologist and have then returned to their own country to practice; others have done some training in their own country and traveled to undertake further postgraduate work. David, who falls into the second category, did the first part of his training in South Africa where the training is at masters level, and then came to the UK to undertake doctoral level work. Because of the changes in South Africa, requiring a further exam, David needed to prepare for this in order to become registered with the

Health Professions Council of South Africa. Below is a brief account of his experience:

As one of three trainee counselling psychologists at the University of Natal in 1999, I trained alongside seven clinical psychologists and five educational psychologists. The training was almost identical, the difference being to do with where students do their internships. I completed my internship at the university's counselling service, whereas the clinical psychology trainees were sent to do theirs at the various local psychiatric hospitals, with the educational psychologists taking up internships in child and family clinics. One of the disadvantages of that training, as I later discovered when I arrived in the UK, was that although the academic content was appropriate, I did not personally achieve a clear professional identity of what it is that differentiates counselling psychology from other applied psychologies. In my training in the UK, however, I finally arrived at a sense of what it is to be a counselling psychologist. Only then did I learn that what distinguished counselling psychology is not the context in which we work, nor is it the type of client we work with, but rather it is to do with the humanistic approach that informs our work, whether that is in the NHS, in organizations, in counselling services or in private practise. While my favoured therapeutic approach is cognitive behavioural therapy, I attempt to practise this in a way that is congruent with the philosophy of counselling psychology. During my stay in the UK I worked for five years in the NHS, as well as completing a doctorate in counselling psychology. The latter experience gave me much more confidence to conduct and review research. I have since returned to South Africa where I am the Head of a University Counselling Centre. One of the joys of working in a centre such as this is that you are able to see a variety of clients, not just the ones that meet strict clinical criteria as is the case in the NHS. My job also involves supervising intern counselling psychologists; I feel much more competent to do this after my UK training and experience. Other differences in working in South Africa compared to the UK are that there is less of an emphasis on evidence-based practice. This gives therapists greater freedom to practise as they see fit, but it also means that the profession has not attained the respect that counselling psychology has attained in the UK. Also, in working in a developing country, I am confronted with misery and anxiety that is the result of poverty and illness. And as a white psychologist working in South Africa, I am still learning to deal sensitively with the many cross-cultural issues that are a common feature of this rapidly changing society. While the professional identities are still not as clear in South Africa, I hope that the intern counselling psychologists who complete their training at the Centre will leave knowing that what defines them is not so much what they do, but rather the way in which this humanistic philosophy informs their work.

This account is interesting in that it suggests a coherent value system across counselling psychologists in different countries, a value system that might be more important than differences in trainings or work settings.

Employment issues in counselling psychology

Counselling psychologists in the UK fought for many years for parity with our clinical psychology colleagues in relation to pay. At that time the NHS had specific 'pay scales' in place for clinical psychologists. Parity was finally granted which, at the time, seemed like an important victory. However, the NHS is currently undergoing reorganization, what is called the Agenda for Change, and as a result all pay scales have been abandoned. Instead, we now have what are called 'pay rates' which are based on a combination of job tasks and competencies. However, these pay rates are the same for both counselling and clinical psychologists, providing us with a kind of parity. Assistant psychologists, trainees, qualified professionals and consultant level have specific starting points; the rates that are still in force at the time of writing range from a starting salary for an assistant psychologist of approximately £15,000 to top salaries of approximately £70,000. One drawback for counselling psychologists who want to work in the NHS is that they are not offered an NHS post as part of their training, a fact which distinguishes them from their clinical psychology colleagues. Many trainee counselling psychologists continue to work on an 'honorarium' or voluntary basis before they are fully qualified as chartered counselling psychologists. Those trainees who do not see themselves as NHS employees, at least on a full-time basis, still need to undertake voluntary placements while at the same time funding their training. This can lead to a preference for part-time study so that a job, perhaps in a different career setting, can be continued for the duration of training. Efforts are currently being made in the UK to achieve training posts in counselling psychology but as yet there has been no agreement about this and each course director, for example, needs to forge their own relationship with local trusts in order to provide any paid opportunities. Pay scales for the Prison Service have been agreed by the Home Office in the UK, and counselling psychologists are able to apply for training posts in that setting. We do not have direct information about pay differentials across different countries. However, with the advent of initiatives such as the European Federation of Psychologists' Associations (EFPA) such information is likely to become more widely available.

6

CURRENT DEBATES AND CHALLENGES IN COUNSELLING PSYCHOLOGY

In this final chapter we summarize a number of the themes that we have previously raised, highlighting these in relation to current and on-going debates in the field. There are considerable changes afoot in the UK, some of these affecting the helping professions as a whole. Of particular interest at present are the proposals for statutory regulation, an issue that has been generating significant stress within applied psychology and in the helping professions in general. We highlight below some of the key elements of these political developments, and some of the questions that they raise. The theme of identity has long been around in this profession and we comment below on the current status of this debate in the context of the boundary with related professions, as well as in relation to training issues. We then return to what we see as some of the key challenges for counselling psychology, concerned, for example, with the requirement to integrate theory, research and practice, and to manage what we call the philosophical conundrum. We conclude with a summary of our perspective on the profession of counselling psychology, based on our experience of this field over a long period, and on the research that we have done for this book. Incorporated into these deliberations are also a number of international themes.

Statutory regulation of the professions

The issue of statutory regulation of the counselling and psychotherapeutic professions has been around in the UK for a long time and has generated much heated debate and related political activity. Writers such as Nick Totton and Richard House have taken up a strong anti-statutory position, rallying professionals to their arguments (e.g. Totton, 1997; House, 2001, 2005). Other writers take up a middle ground position, recognizing some of the anti-statutory arguments but presenting a broader analysis of professional activity, either in terms of the sociology of the professions, or in terms of some of the more nonsensical elements of professional activity and so-called progress. The notion of 'expertise' and its manifestation within the fields of applied psychology has been well documented by Cheshire and Pilgrim (2004) who offer an analysis, with particular reference to the profession of clinical psychology, of the professions as examples of particular interest groups located within a social system. From such a standpoint, an assessment of what constitutes a particular professional group, its purpose as well as its relationship with its 'clients', takes on a more complex perspective, as does the notion of 'the protection of the public', a key issue behind the move towards regulation. Pilgrim (2005) considers two particular aspects of professionalism which relate directly to the question of statutory regulation, the issues of professional activities as 'sites of risk', and the relationship between 'competence and effectiveness' (pp. 171–172). His approach to the question of risk is framed in cost-benefit terms, involving an analysis of the tension between gain and cost in therapeutic activity, and the assessment and control of negative risk. He highlights the power implications of a professional group's position in portraying both its worth to the public as well as its ability to police danger, taking a somewhat sceptical view of these claims. In his discussion of the relationship between competence and effectiveness he highlights the importance both of relational and moral aspects of therapeutic activity proposing that 'given the centrality of the relationship to the success or failure of therapy, technique is worth nothing unless it is underpinned consistently with a positive, respectful and non-abusive stance towards the client. Personal integrity, not just technical competence, must be reliably present in the therapy trade' (p. 172). Pilgrim goes on to question whether professional registration is the right vehicle for the promotion or policing of such qualities and concludes that there is little evidence to suggest that this way forward will meet those requirements.

Craig Newnes, in his inimitable style, brings out the absurdity of our professional activities and claims (Newnes, 2007a) highlighting the difficulty of monitoring any activity, such as therapy, which is based on a 'conversation', which as he points out, can move in a number of different directions. He puts forward the view that:

> [N]o system of registration or practice based on researching what others claim to do or achieve in therapy can guarantee that your therapist's chosen modus operandum will lead to change in the desired direction. Neither a registered therapist nor a well researched therapy can create

the necessary conditions for you to concentrate on your various therapy homework assignments. Nor can the therapist move beyond self interest. (p. 223)

In that article Newnes is addressing issues arising from *The Depression Report* (Layard et al., 2007) which highlights the economic implications of depression and the claim that the situation can be alleviated by the implementation of brief, CBT-based therapeutic interventions. Newnes is sceptical of the claims in this report, with its focus on getting people back to work. He states:

the Depression Report isn't about people feeling better, moving on, self actualising or the rest. It's about claiming to get people back to work and off benefits. Someone with a potentially life-changing spell of madness or mortifying sense of anomie will be funnelled into a job with the kind of pay and conditions of service the therapist left behind long ago. Therapists in Layard's brave new world become an arm of the state-serving bourgeoisie in a far more explicit way than before. In effect, they are paid by the State to make sure people remain cogs in the machine rather than giving them a collective voice on the parlous state of modern society. (p. 227)

We can discern in these debates the rather grave existential issues embedded in our society and currently being expressed through economic and legislative mechanisms.

At the time of writing, however, the issue of statutory regulation seems to have been resolved in favour of state registration, not a surprising outcome. The UK Department of Health favours the extension of its Health Professions Council (HPC) as the statutory body to regulate the profession of psychology. The BPS is currently in consultation with the HPC on the terms and conditions of registration and the details surrounding the potentially protected title of 'Practitioner Psychologist'. Official registration is currently set to begin early in 2009, with suitable grandparenting clauses in place for a specified period of time. It is anticipated that the next step will be the regulation of psychotherapists and counsellors and the UK Council for Psychotherapy (UKCP) is already making plans to take account of such developments. In the wider global field it is evident that statutory regulation of the psychological therapies has been seen as the obvious way forward, even though, as we have outlined in relation to the position of psychotherapists in Germany, there are a number of serious difficulties and criticisms that still need to be addressed. We are not surprised by these developments in terms of the zealous motivation of state control, but would support the more creative critical perspectives of several of our colleagues as crucial in the ensuring of a more adequate service to clients. Counselling psychology as a profession has a key role to play in these developments, given its somewhat anarchic style and its commitment to a set of humanistic principles.

Professional identities

A key area of concern in counselling psychology has historically been in the development and maintenance of its own identity in the context of the BPS family of applied psychologies. As we have previously highlighted, historically, counselling psychology needed to fight hard for its identity as a separate profession, the central aspect being the location of its philosophy and practices within a humanistic paradigm which emphasizes the importance of subjective and intersubjective perspectives. Early trainings in counselling psychology in the UK probably had a clearer identity from a philosophical point of view. However, what we have seen in the UK is a growing interest for counselling psychologists to work in the National Health Service (NHS) alongside clinical psychologists and psychiatrists, with the attendant requirement to work with more severely disturbed patients, many of whom will also be on medication of various kinds. Within that setting there is also a tradition of the use of psychological tests as well as others for organic problems such as memory function. This has inevitably led to a debate in counselling psychology about the nature of the curriculum and whether it covered all areas that a chartered counselling psychologist might need for employment purposes. The conclusion reached following significant deliberations within the profession was that the curriculum in counselling psychology should be extended to include a greater focus on psychopathology, an understanding of psychopharmacology and its relevance to the therapeutic context, and knowledge and expertise in the use of psychological tests relevant to the therapeutic endeavour. All of these areas are now represented in the competency framework for the profession. In the discussions leading up to the inclusion of these areas in the competency framework there was much heated debate, with concerns especially about moving closer to the medical model which dominates the NHS. At the same time it became clear that counselling psychology brought a refreshing approach to the debates, raising important issues related to the tension between structure and process. For example, in a special edition of the *Counselling Psychology Review* in 2004, which included international perspectives, all contributors managed to convey the potential usefulness of tests while maintaining a critical perspective on this form of 'knowledge' and locating the using of tests within a process-based and humanistic framework (e.g. Van Scoyoc, 2004).

However, it is also true that the inclusion of these new areas in the counselling psychology curriculum represents a move towards less distinction between counselling psychologists and clinical psychologists in terms of professional identity. While counselling psychologists often claim the humanistic and reflexive ground as the value added piece in this profession, we consider that this can rather caricature the average clinical psychologist as not interested in subjectivity or humanistic values, a fact which does not stand up in reality. It would appear that there is increasingly more convergence than divergence between the different helping professions, although we can imagine that for the average patient or client with a problem some of the issues might simply appear confusing. Consider, for example, the debate about the difference between counselling and psychotherapy. While we would not view these professional realms as necessarily exclusive of each other, this distinction does seem to hold historically in terms of the development of counselling psychology in different countries around the world, and is also a distinction which has been debated within professional accrediting bodies in the UK. Within the BPS itself we have counselling psychology as a speciality, but we now also have the Register of Psychologists Specialising in Psychotherapy, a register that is cross-divisional and whose members include both counselling and clinical psychologists. This register was designed to reflect post-qualification and post-chartered status, shifting the goal posts another notch higher.

Historically, the fields of counselling and psychotherapy could be viewed as having different roots, with Carl Rogers often identified with the beginning of the counselling movement and Sigmund Freud with the starting point in psychoanalysis of more broad-based psychotherapeutic approaches designed perhaps to consider more serious presenting issues as conceived within the medical model. Also, in many of the settings that we reviewed in Chapter 1, it was clear that a distinction could be made between the emphasis on the importance of relationship within the therapeutic settings, and a focus, for example, on problem-solving and decision-making skills. We can see that some versions of counselling psychology are rooted in the guidance tradition of advice giving rather than in the subjective and intersubjective domain with the focus on relational factors. From the perspective of counselling psychology, it is evident that practitioners may work in different ways, depending on their training background, the particular speciality that they have pursued, and the context that they choose to work in. Also, as Clarkson and Pokorny (1994) points out, in reflecting on differences between different professional titles and related territorial anxieties, 'issues of power, ideology, money, status, employability and snobbery play a significant part' (p. 7).

The political arena and training considerations

A number of recent political developments the UK, prompted partly by a consideration of economic factors as well as by the move towards statutory regulation, have raised some significant challenges relevant to all of the helping professions. A significant challenge came in 2004 with the publication of Lord Layard's policy paper on the cost of mental health problems to the UK economy (Layard, 2004). This paper, written from an economist's point of view, concerned itself with ways in which people with mental health problems might be 'cured' as quickly as possible, and returned to the world of work. The proposal was that these people should be offered brief psychological therapy of the cognitive behavioural kind, the latter being highlighted as having a particularly strong evidence base. While we have previously drawn attention to the much more complex and less definitive views which have emerged from the research literature on different therapeutic approaches, this political paper set the tone for Cognitive Behaviour Therapy (CBT) as the treatment of choice within the health service. A paper published in 2004 by the Department of Health in the UK acknowledged that although there was a strong evidence base for CBT there was also research evidence to support the effectiveness of a wide range of therapeutic approaches (Department of Health, 2004). More recent developments, however, make it clear that the Department of Health is promoting CBT as the preferred option, with a particular focus on presenting problems of depression and anxiety (e.g. Department of Health, 2007).

A second and parallel development at national level in the UK has been the establishment of the Skills for Health programme with the objective of setting national occupational standards for the psychological therapies. The tendency in this drive is to define effectiveness in relation to traditional and positivistic approaches to research with the random controlled trial as the gold standard, paralleling the medical model. There is currently much discussion about these developments with different groups lobbying for their own agendas, and fostering a competitive rather than a collaborative environment. At the time of writing, counselling psychology is very much a part of these debates but it remains to be seen how far the political juggernaut can be tackled, at least as far as the NHS is concerned. Nonetheless, we appear to have humanistic approaches confirmed as a separate category of psychological therapy although the national occupational standards for this orientation have yet to be explicitly defined.

A somewhat different challenge, although also emanating from the dominance of the NHS, raises issues about the training of applied psychologists in relation in particular to service delivery in mental health. In a recent paper Peter Kinderman, a clinical psychologist, put forward a perspective on the training of applied psychologists, suggesting that the present system of differentiating across different applied psychology domains should be radically rethought (Kinderman, 2005). A system of different levels of education is proposed, with level one focusing on the undergraduate domain, level two on short-term training of psychology graduates who would be called 'associate psychologists', and level three focusing on more specialist training to doctoral level. These ideas were incorporated into a wider framework which considers more practical ways of approaching applied psychology training (BPS, 2007e). More debate is needed, but at this time, we find it is difficult to see how a comprehensive training programme for counselling psychology could be 'reduced' to a common denominator of some kind with only one year of specialization. Some of these ideas are nonetheless being pursued in terms of potential plans for the Health Professions Council (HPC) to register associate psychologists. It is our view that we have some way to go before the final picture emerges. In our research and discussions about these developments for this particular chapter we have to acknowledge occasionally feeling glad that we classify ourselves as 'oldies' in this profession and can increasingly rely on some of our younger colleagues to continue the fight. Our feeling also is that it would indeed be very sad to see counselling psychology training as a production line for the NHS. As previously outlined, other countries around the world face similar challenges in the development of the profession, and the need to tackle the issue of what constitutes effectiveness in the psychological therapies.

Key issues in theory, practice and research

We become much more energized about this professional field when we extricate ourselves from the endless political manoeuvrings and think about the creative ideas that the profession has fostered. A key challenge we think lies in the more coherent integration of theory, practice and research than has hitherto been the case. These three areas have traditionally proceeded separately, with theoretical developments divorced from practice considerations and client-based concerns. On the theory front, trainees have had to work out what to do with the range of theoretical ideas presented during their training and how these translate into the domain of the consulting room. It is not enough to take the theoretical pieces and simply apply these in a simplistic way, since this leads to a rather technique-driven approach. For example, both of us have on occasion come across exam scripts where a trainee states a variant of 'I thought that the client seemed sad so I offered some empathy', or 'I thought I'd try a relaxation technique as the client seemed anxious'. One of us (Vanja) can be seen in teaching sessions caricaturing the body position of the 'therapist' with head to one side, gaze firmly set on the client's eyes, accompanied by a gently nodding movement of the head and grunts of 'uh huh'. It takes time and a lot of practice to move beyond the taking on of theoretical ideas and internalizing these in a fashion which provides the client with the coherent and authentic experience necessary for change to occur. Turning to a consideration of research, this activity is often divorced from practice and at risk of being a rather fragmented pursuit. More recent perspectives on research activities, focusing, for example, on 'practice-based evidence', together with the emergence of the practitioner doctorate, allows for much more attention to be paid to the integration of research and practice. Such an emphasis is both radical and exciting in terms of the potential influence within higher education. There is further work to be done, however, since the articulation of practice knowledge is a complex affair, as is the convincing of some universities that there may be a viable alternative to the 'PhD'. Also, a realigning of psychology with philosophy is essential if we are to achieve some useful goals in the educational context.

We also need to address the issue of cultural difference in a much more focused way and think about the implications for the range of ideas expressed through the training requirements. Most of our theories in the psychological therapies have been developed by white western males (most of these now dead!). Likewise, therapeutic techniques that emanate from these theories tend to reflect a similar cultural bias. For example, the question of eye contact and how this is managed is very different in UK/USA settings from that, say, in Japan. In an interesting study which examined counselling style and perceived effectiveness, the researchers compared the perceived effectiveness of counsellors from the perspective of two different cultural groups (D'Rozario and Romano, 2000). The study asked USA and

Singaporean college students to rate videotaped counselling sessions where the counsellors used either a directive or nondirective approach. The results showed that the nondirective style was rated as more 'expert' by the Singaporean students, with the USA students giving higher ratings to the directive counsellor. The researchers expressed surprise at this outcome, since they would have predicted the results to be the other way round. However, the key learning from studies such as this highlights the importance of embedded assumptions which may not fit particular cultural groups and which need to be made explicit and challenged.

David Smail is fiercely critical of psychology's track record in contributing to our understanding of social factors and in translating this understanding into our practices, stating that '[F]or much of psychology, what goes on in the world, what the material relations are between individual and society, are matters of complete irrelevance' (2007, p. 134). While not conveying an allegiance to the existence of an ultimate reality he makes the observation that the credible world is not the same as the real one, thus drawing our attention to the importance of human experience. He writes cogently about the 'inner world' that is so important to all of us, encouraging psychology to be interested in the inner world of individuals in a way which goes beyond our reductionist diagnostic paradigms. His view is that

> ... psychology has imposed on our subjectivity an entirely inappropriate normativeness, a narrow set of moral and aesthetic prescriptions which turns each of us into a kind of self-diagnosing psychiatric inquisitor, ready to infer from the recognition of each new feeling pathological deviance from an ideal we think we see embodied in everyone else. (p. 141)

Smail's plea for psychology is to bring a greater focus to the relationship between the inner and the outer in the promotion of a more integrated perspective between personal concerns and the wider environment.

Perspectives on the profession of counselling psychology

And so we reach the final section of this book and offer some general perceptions on the field of counselling psychology and its future, as well as considering our own experiences of putting this book together. When we started on this project we thought that it would be a fairly straightforward venture. We are both senior people in the field and have first-hand experience of the issues that face the profession; we had the initial idea that it would simply be a case of putting down the many things we already knew. In the event, like any useful creative project, we were to be challenged as well as pleasantly surprised. Our research revealed a wealth of information on a global perspective which shook us out of our more context-dominated position and challenged us to have a new look at the profession of counselling psychology, its values and assumptions, and the ways that these had been interpreted from a more global point of view. We have also discovered that it is not the professional identity and 'turf' related concerns that matter, but the commitment to a certain set of philosophical ideas that is important. Our researches have brought us closer to our colleagues in other professions, turning the idea of collaboration as an intellectual nicety to an absolute necessity in the current political climate. We have become much more aware of some of the madness in our personal debates, as well as the broader madness in discussions, for example, of psychopathology and in discussions about how to deal with this. At times we have connected with a slightly more absurd quality which comes out of these discussions. Newnes (2007b), for example, draws attention to some of the absurdities in the field of the psychological therapies, borrowing from Spike Milligan and stating that '[M]adness is in the eye of the beholder – get it out with Optrex' (p. 192). And of course there is a serious side to these debates considering the power of political processes and the constant need to fight for some different ways of seeing and experiencing. We believe that counselling psychology as a profession has a large amount of knowledge and practice to contribute to current debates and to the formulation of policy in relation to the development of the psychological therapies. We hope that what we have offered in this book will support the confidence of practitioners to speak out in favour of what is important both for clients and for the profession, while retaining a close watch on their own competitive or narcissistic parts that are likely to fight for turf and exclusion.

RELEVANT CONTACT INFORMATION

The British Psychological Society
St Andrews House
48 Princess Road East
Leicester, LE1 7DR
Tel: +44(0)116 254 9568
www.bps.org.uk

Information on how to train as a BPS recognized chartered counselling psychologist can be obtained directly from the BPS or on
www.bps.org.uk/careers

For details of whether you are eligible for GBR as a UK or overseas
graduate contact the BPS or look on www.bps.org.uk/membership/
grades/gbr1.cfm

BPS training routes in counselling psychology:
www.bps.org.uk/dcop/cources.cfm

BPS Division of Counselling Psychology:
www.bps.org.uk/dcop/dcop_home.cfm

BPS Division of Counselling Psychology – Scotland:
www.bps.org.uk/dcop/cops/cops_home.cfm

BPS Division of Counselling Psychology – Wales:
www.bps.org.uk/dcop/wales/wales_home.cfm

BPS requirements for Continuing Professional Development
(CPD):
www.bps.org.uk/professional-development/cpd/cpd_index.cfm

BPS Division of Clinical Psychology and other divisions, special
interest groups etc:
www.bps.org.uk/networks/networks_home.cfm

Health Professions Council (HPC)
Park House

184 Kennington Park Road
London, SE11 4BU
www.hpc-uk.org

NHS careers information and pay scales
www.nhscareers.nhs.uk/details/Default.aspx?Id=446

The Quality Assurance Agency for UK Higher Education (QAA)
You can find descriptors for the different levels of higher education
at: www.qaa.ac.uk/

British Association for Counselling and Psychotherapy (BACP)
BACP House
15 St John's Business Park
Lutterworth, LE17 4HB
www.bacp.co.uk

UK Council for Psychotherapy (UKCP)
2nd Floor, Edward House
2 Wakley Street
London, EC1V 7LT
info@psychotherapy.org.uk
www.psychotherapy.org.uk

The Psychological Society of Ireland (PSI)
CX House, 2A Corn Exchange Place
Poolbeg Street
Dublin 2, Ireland
info@psihq.ie
www.psihq.ie

The American Psychological Association (APA)
750 First Street, NE,
Washington, DC 20002–4242, USA
www.apa.org

Canadian Psychological Association (CPA)
141 Laurier Avenue West, Suite 702
Ottawa, Ontario K1P 5J3, Canada
cpa@cpa.ca
www.cpa.ca

USA and Canada: information about licensure
www.asppb.org

The Korean Counselling Psychological Association (KCPA)
www.krcpa.or.kr

Australian Psychological Society (APS)
www.psychology.org.au

New Zealand Psychological Association (NZPA)
www.psychology.org.nz

Hong Kong Psychological Society's newest division is that of counselling psychology formed in 2006.
For details go to www.hkps.org.hk/www/

Chinese Psychological Society formed the Committee of Clinical
and Counselling Psychology in 2001.
www.cpsbeijing.org/

Professional Board for Psychology of the Health Professions
Council of South Africa
www.hpcsa.co.za

The International Association of Applied Psychology (IAAP)
www.iaapcounselingpsychology.org

European Association for Counselling Psychology (EACP)
www.counselling-psychology.eu/

European Association for Psychotherapy (EAP)
www.europsyche.org

European Federation of Psychologists' Associations (EFPA)
www.efpa.com

REFERENCES

Alilovic, K. (2007). 'Practice what you preach'. A day in the life of an academic counselling psychologist. *Counselling Psychology Review, 22*(1), 5–7.

Alker, L. P., & Cooper, C. (2007). The complexities of undertaking counselling evaluation in the workplace. *Counselling Psychology Quarterly, 20*(2), 177–190.

Alvesson, M., & Sköldberg, K. (2000). *Reflexive methodology: new vistas for qualitative research.* London: Sage.

American Psychological Association, Division of Counseling and Guidance, Committee on Definition (1956). Counseling psychology as a specialty. *American Psychologist, 11*, 282–285.

American Psychiatric Association (2000). *Diagnostic and Statistical Manual of Mental Disorders – text revision (DSM-IV-TR).* Washington DC: American Psychiatric Association.

Andrews, G., & Harvey, R. (1981). Does psychotherapy benefit neurotic patients: A re-analysis of the Smith, Glass & Miller data. *Archives of General Psychiatry, 38*, 1203–1208.

Argyris, C. (1970). *Intervention theory and method: a behavioral science view.* Reading, MA: Addison-Wesley.

Argyris, C. (2004). *Reasons and rationalizations: the limits to organizational knowledge.* Oxford: Oxford University Press.

Arulmani, G. (2007). Counselling psychology in India: at the confluence of two traditions. *Applied Psychology: An International Review, 56*(1), 69–82.

Assagioli, R. (1975). *Psychosynthesis.* Wellingborough: Turnstone Press.

Assagioli, R. (1976). *Transpersonal inspiration and psychological mountain climbing.* New York: Psychosynthesis Research Foundation.

Bandura, A. (1977). *Social learning theory.* Englewood Cliffs, NJ: Prentice-Hall.

Barkham, M. (2007). Methods, outcomes and processes in the psychological therapies across four successive research generations. In W. Dryden (Ed.), *Dryden's handbook of individual therapy* (5th Ed.). London: Sage.

Barkham, M., & Mellor-Clark, J. (2003). Bridging evidence-based practice and practice-based evidence: developing a rigorous and relevant knowledge for the psychological therapies. *Clinical Psychology and Psychotherapy, 10*, 319–327.

Barrom, C. P., Shadish, W. R., & Montgomery, L. M. (1988). PhDs, PsyDs and real-world constraints on scholarly activity: another look at the Boulder Model. *Professional Psychology: Research and Practice, 19*, 93–101.

Beck, A. T. (1963). Thinking and depression: 1. idiosyncratic content and cognitive distortions. *Archives of General Psychiatry, 9*, 324–333.

Beck, A. T. (1964). Thinking and depression: 2. theory and therapy. *Archives of General Psychiatry, 10*, 561–571.

Beck, A. T. (1972). *Depression: causes and treatment.* Philadelphia: University of Pennsylvania Press.

Beck, A. T., Freeman, A., Davis, D. D., & associates (2003). *Cognitive therapy of personality disorders* (2nd Ed.). New York: Guilford Press.

Beebe, B., Knoblauch, S., Rustin, J., & Sorter, D. (2005). *Forms of intersubjectivity in infant research and adult treatment.* New York: Other Press.

Beebe, B., & Lachmann, F. M. (2002). *Infant research and adult treatment.* Hillsdale, NJ: The Analytic Press.

Bekerman, Z., & Tatar, M. (2005). Overcoming modern-postmodern dichotomies: some possible benefits for the counselling profession. *British Journal of Guidance and Counselling, 33*(3), 411–421.

Belar, C. D. (2000). Scientist-Practitioner ≠ Science + Practice. *American Psychologist, 55,* 249–250.

Belar, C. D., & Perry, N. W. (1992). National conference on scientist-practitioner education and training for the professional practice of psychology. *American Psychologist, 47,* 71–75.

Benjamin, B. A. (2007). Counselling psychology in Israel: a virtual specialty in transition. *Applied Psychology: An International Review, 56*(1), 83–96.

Berger, P., & Luckmann, T. (1966). *The social construction of reality: a treatise in the sociology of knowledge.* New York: Penguin Books.

Bernaud, J., Cohen-Scali, V., & Guichard, J. (2007). Counseling psychology in France: a paradoxical situation. *Applied Psychology: An International Review, 56*(1), 131–151.

Berne, E. (1986). *Transactional analysis in psychotherapy.* London: Souvenir Press. (First published in 1961.)

Blackham, H. J. (1952). *Six existentialist thinkers.* New York: Harper Torchbooks.

Boring, E. (1957). *A history of experimental psychology* (2nd Ed.). New York: Appleton Century-Crofts.

Bowen, M. (1985). *Family therapy in clinical practice.* Northvale, NJ: Aronson.

Bowman, C. E., & Nevis, E. C. (2005). The history and development of gestalt therapy. In Woldt, A. L., & Toman, S. L. (Eds.), *Gestalt therapy: history, theory, and practice.* Thousand Oaks, CA: Sage.

Brazier, D. (1995). *Zen therapy: a Buddhist approach to psychotherapy.* London: Constable.

British Psychological Society (2005a). *Division of counselling psychology: professional practice guidelines.* Leicester: BPS.

British Psychological Society (2005b). *Criteria for the accreditation of doctoral training programmes in counselling psychology.* Leicester: BPS.

British Psychological Society (2006). *Code of ethics and conduct.* Leicester: BPS.

British Psychological Society (2007a). Definition of counselling psychology retrieved from www.bps.org.uk/careers/society_qual/counselling.cfm

British Psychological Society (2007b). *Child protection portfolio.* Leicester: BPS.

British Psychological Society (2007c). *Psychologists as expert witnesses: guidelines and procedures for England and Wales.* Leicester: BPS.

British Psychological Society (2007d). *Statement on the conduct of psychologists providing expert psychometric evidence to courts and lawyers.* Leicester: BPS Psychological Testing Centre.

British Psychological Society (2007e). *New ways of working for applied psychologists in health and social care: models of training.* Leicester: BPS.

British Psychological Society Professional Affairs Board (1980). *Counselling: the report of a working party.* Leicester: BPS.

Broad, C. D. (1975). *Leibniz: an introduction.* Cambridge: Cambridge University Press.

Brown, J., & Corne, L. (2004). Counselling psychology in Australia. *Counselling Psychology Quarterly, 17*(3), 287–299.

Buber, M. (1970). *I and thou* (W. Kaufmann, trans.). Edinburgh: T. T. Clark.

Bugental, J. F. T. (1965). *The search for authenticity: an existential-analytic approach to psychotherapy.* New York: Holt, Rinehart & Winston.

Carroll, M. (1996). *Counselling supervision: theory, skills and practice*. London: Cassell.

Castonguay, L. G., Goldfried, M. R., Wiser, S., & Raue, P. J. (1996). Predicting the effect of cognitive therapy for depression: A study of unique and common factors. *Journal of Consulting and Clinical Psychology, 64*, 497–504.

Chaiklin, S. (1992). From theory to practice and back again: what does postmodern philosophy contribute to psychological science? In S. Kvale (Ed.) *Psychology and postmodernism*. London: Sage.

Chang, D. F., Tong, H. Q., Shi, Q. J., & Zeng, Q. F. (2005). Letting a hundred flowers bloom: counseling and psychotherapy in the People's Republic of China. *Journal of Mental Health Counseling, 27*, 104–116.

Cheshire, K., & Pilgrim, D. (2004). *A short introduction to clinical psychology*. London: Sage.

Clarkson, P., & Pokorny, M. (Eds.) (1994). *The handbook of psychotherapy*. London and New York: Routledge.

Clifford, J. (1996). Adlerian therapy. In W. Dryden (Ed.), *Handbook of individual therapy*. London: Sage.

Cohn, H. W. (1997). *Existential thought and therapeutic practice: an introduction to existential psychotherapy*. London: Sage.

Cooper, M. (2003). *Existential therapies*. London: Sage.

Corney, R. (2003). Counselling psychology in primary care settings. In R. Woolfe, W. Dryden & S. Strawbridge (Eds.), *Handbook of counselling psychology*. London: Sage.

Corrie S., & Callanan M. M. (2001). Therapists' beliefs about research and the scientist-practitioner model in evidence-based health care climate: a qualitative study. *British Journal of Medical Psychology, 74*, 135–149.

Cottingham, J. G. (1986). *Descartes*. Oxford: Blackwell.

Crits-Christoph, P., & Mintz, J. (1991). Implications of therapist effects for the design and analysis of comparative studies of psychotherapies. *Journal of Consulting and Clinical Psychology, 59*, 20–26.

Cunningham, S. (2004). *Informing strategic planning: a needs assessment of members of the Division of Counselling Psychology of the Psychological Society of Ireland*. Unpublished masters thesis, University of Dublin, Trinity College, Dublin, Ireland.

Danziger, K. (1985). The origins of the psychological experiment as a social institution. *American Psychologist, 40*, 133–140.

Danziger, K. (1990). *Constructing the subject: historical origins of psychological research*. Cambridge: Cambridge University Press.

Danziger, K. (1997). *Naming the mind: how psychology found its language*. London: Sage.

Derrida, J. (1978). *Writing and difference* (A. Bass, trans.). Chicago: University of Chicago Press.

Department of Health (2004). *Organising and delivering psychological therapies*. www.dh.gov.uk

Department of Health (2007). *Cognitive and behavioural therapy for people with anxiety and depression: what skills can service users expect their therapists to have?* www.dh.gov.uk

Desmond, A., & Moore, J. (1991). *Darwin*. London: Michael Joseph.

DeYoung, P. A. (2003). *Relational psychotherapy: a primer*. New York and Hove: Brunner-Routledge.

Diagnostic and Statistical Manual of Mental Disorders: text revision (DSM-IV-TR) (2000). Washington, DC: American Psychiatric Association.

Dobson, K. S. (2002). A national imperative: public funding of psychological services. *Canadian Psychology, 43*(2), 65–75, May.

Doll, E. A. (1946). The divisional structure of the APA. *American Psychologist, 1*, 336–345.

Donati, M., & Watts, M. (2000). Personal development in counselling psychology training: the case for further research. *Counselling Psychology Review, 15*(1), 12–21.

D'Rozario, V., & Romano, J. L. (2000). Perceptions of counsellor effectiveness: A study of two country groups. *Counselling Psychology Quarterly, 13*(1), 51–63.

Dryden, W. (1996). Rational emotive behaviour therapy. In W. Dryden (Ed.), *Handbook of individual therapy.* London: Sage.

du Plock, S. (2006). Just what is it that makes contemporary counselling psychology so different, so appealing? *Counselling Psychology Review, 21*(3), 22–32.

Duarte, M. E., Paixão, M. P., & Lima, M. R. (2007). Perspectives on counseling psychology: Portugal at a glance. *Applied Psychology: An International Review, 56*(1), 119–130.

Efran, J. S., & Clarfield, L. E. (1992). Constructionist therapy: sense and nonsense. In S. McNamee & K. J. Gergen (Eds.), *Therapy as social construction.* London: Sage.

Elliott, M. S., & Williams, D. I. (2002). A qualitative evaluation of an employee counselling service from the perspective of client, counsellor and organization. *Counselling Psychology Quarterly, 15*(2), 201–208.

Ellis, A. (1976). The biological basis of human irrationality. *Journal of Individual Psychology, 32,* 145–168.

Ellis, A., & Harper, R. A. (1975). *A new guide to rational living.* North Hollywood, CA: Wilshire.

Ellis, A., & Whiteley, J. M. (Eds.) (1979). *Theoretical and empirical foundations of rational-emotive therapy.* Monterey, CA: Brooks Cole.

Elton Wilson, J., & Barkham, M. (1994). A practitioner approach to psychotherapy process and outcome research. In P. Clarkson & M. Pokorny (Eds.), *Handbook of psychotherapy.* London: Routledge.

Epstein, M. (1996). *Thoughts without a thinker: psychotherapy from a Buddhist perspective.* London: Duckworth.

Etherington, K. (2004). *Becoming a reflexive researcher: using our selves in research.* London: Jessica Kingsley Publishers.

European Association of Psychotherapy (EAP) (1990). Strasbourg Declaration on Psychotherapy of 1990. www.psychother.com/esp stras-decl.htm

European Federation of Psychologists' Associations (EFPA) (1990). *Optimal standards for professional training in psychology.* www.efpa.be

Eysenck, H. J. (1952). The effects of psychotherapy: an evaluation. *Journal of Consulting Psychology, 16,* 319–324.

Farr, R. (1983). Wilhelm Wundt and the origins of psychology as an experimental and social science. *British Journal of Social Psychology, 22,* 289–381.

Feyerabend, P. (1987). *Farewell to reason.* London and New York: Verso.

Fleck, L. (1979). *The genesis and development of a scientific fact.* Chicago: University of Chicago Press.

Fonagy, P., Gergely, G., Jurist, E. L., & Target, M. (2004). *Affect regulation, mentalization, and the development of the self.* London: Karnac.

Foucault, M. (2001). *Madness and civilization: a history of insanity in the age of reason* (R. Howard, trans.). London and New York: Routledge.

Frank, J. D., & Frank, J. B. (1961). *Persuasion and healing: a comparative study of psychotherapy.* Baltimore, MD: The John Hopkins University Press.

Frank, P. (1949). *Modern science and its philosophy.* Cambridge, MA: Harvard University Press.

Frankland, A. (2007). Counselling psychology: the trade for the portfolio professional. *Counselling Psychology Review, 22*(1), 41–45.

Fransella, F., & Dalton, P. (1996). Personal construct therapy. In W. Dryden (Ed.), *Handbook of individual therapy.* London: Sage.

Freud, S. (1912). Recommendations for physicians on the psycho-analytic method of treatment. *Collected Papers, Volume 2.* (J. Riviere, trans.). New York: Basic Books.

Freud, S. (1949). *An outline of psychoanalysis.* (J. Strachey, trans.). London: Hogarth Press.

Freud, S. (1950). Project for a scientific psychology. In *The standard edition of the complete psychological works of Sigmund Freud (Vol. 1)* (J. Strachey, trans.). London: Hogarth Press.

Freud, S. (1960). *The letters of Sigmund Freud.* New York: Basic Books.

Gelso, C. J. (2006). On the making of a scientist-practitioner: a theory of research training in professional psychology. *Training and Education in Professional Psychology, S,* 3–16.

Gay, P. (Ed.) (1995). *The Freud reader.* London: Vintage. (Originally published in 1989 by W. W. Norton & Company Inc.)

Gelso, C. J., & Fretz, B. R. (2001). *Counseling Psychology* (2nd Ed.). Fort Worth, TX: Harcourt College.

Georgopoulou, V. (2007). A week in the life of a counselling psychologist in a CAMHS context. *Counselling Psychologist Review, 22*(1), 11–18.

Giddens, A. (1987). *Social theory and modern sociology.* Cambridge: Polity Press.

Giddens, A. (1991). *Modernity and self-identity: self and society in the late modern age.* Cambridge: Polity Press.

Gilbert, M. C., & Evans, K. (2000). *Psychotherapy supervision: an integrative relational approach to psychotherapy supervision.* Buckingham: Open University Press..

Goffman, E. (1968). *Stigma: notes on the management of spoiled identity.* Harmandsworth: Penguin Books. (First published in 1963.)

Gold, M. (Ed.) (1999). *The complete social scientist: a Kurt Lewin reader.* Washington, DC: American Psychological Association.

Goldfried, M. R., & Eubanks-Carter, C. (2004). On the need for a new psychotherapy research paradigm: Comment on Westen, Novotny, and Thompson-Brenner. *Psychological Bulletin, 130,* 669–673.

Goldfried, M. R., & Wolfe, B. E. (1996). Psychotherapy practice and research: repairing a strained alliance. *American Psychologist, 51,* 1007–1016.

Gomez, L. (1997). *An introduction to object relations.* London: Free Association Books.

Grant, B. (1999). Walking on a rackety bridge: mapping supervision. Paper presented to the *HERDSA Annual International Conference,* Melbourne, July.

Greenberg, L. S., Rice, L. N., & Elliott, R. (1993). *Facilitating emotional change: the moment-by-moment process.* New York: the Guilford Press.

Greenberg, J. R., & Mitchell, S. A. (1983). *Object relations in psychoanalytic theory.* Cambridge, MA: Harvard University Press.

Greenberg, L., Watson, J., & Lietaer, G. (Eds.) (1999). *Handbook of experiential psychotherapy.* New York: The Guilford Press.

Hall, J. A. (1986). *The Jungian experience: analysis and individuation.* Toronto, Canada: Inner City Books.

Hammersley, D. (2003). Training and professional development in the context of counselling psychology. In R. Woolfe, W. Dryden & S. Strawbridge (Eds.), *Handbook of counselling psychology* (2nd Ed.). London: Sage.

Handy, C. (1989). *The age of unreason.* London: Random House.

Hannan, N. (2001). *The practice of counselling psychology in Ireland: a profile.* Unpublished masters thesis, University of Dublin, Trinity College, Dublin, Ireland.

Hargaden, H., & Sills, C. (2002). *Transactional analysis: a relational perspective.* East Sussex: Brunner-Routledge.

Hawkins, P., & Shohet, R. (2000). *Supervision in the helping professions.* Buckingham: Open University Press.

Heidegger, M. (1962). *Being and time* (J. Macquarrie & E. Robinson, trans.). Oxford: Blackwell.

Heppner, P. P., Wampold, B. E., & Kivlighan Jr, D. M. (2008). *Research design in counselling* (3rd Ed.). Belmont, CA: Thomson Brooks/Cole.

Holloway, E. (1995). *Clinical supervision: a systems approach.* Thousand Oaks, CA: Sage.

Homans, P. (1989). *The ability to mourn: disillusionment and the social origins of psychoanalysis.* Chicago and London: The University of Chicago Press.

Hoshmand, L. T., & Polkinghorne, D. E. (1992). Redefining the science-practice relationship and professional training. *American Psychologist, 47*(1), 55–66.

Hou, Z., & Zhang, N. (2007). Counseling Psychology in China. *Applied Psychology: An International Review, 56*(1), 33–50.

House, R. (2001). Psychotherapy professionalization: The post-graduate dimension and the legitimacy of statutory regulation. *British Journal of Psychotherapy, 17*(3), 382–390.

House, R. (2005). The state regulation of counselling and psychotherapy: sometime, never …? *Journal of Critical Psychology, Counselling and Psychotherapy, 5*(4), 176–189.

Jacobs, M. (1986). *The presenting past: An introduction to practical psychodynamic counselling.* Milton Keynes: Open University Press.

Jacobs, M. (1988). *Psychodynamic counselling in action.* London: Sage.

Jørgensen, C. R. (2004). Active ingredients in individual psychotherapy: searching for common factors. *Psychoanalytic Psychology, 21*(4), 516–540.

Jung, C. G. (1969). *The archetypes and the collective unconscious* (2nd Ed.), (R. F. C. Hull, trans.). Princeton, NJ: Princeton University Press.

Kahn, M. (1991). *Between therapist and client: the new relationship.* New York: W. H. Freeman and Company.

Kazdin, A. E. (1986). Comparative outcome studies of psychotherapy: methodological issues and strategies. *Journal of Consulting and Clinical Psychology, 54,* 95–105.

Kelly, G. A. (1963). *A theory of personality: the psychology of personal constructs.* New York: W. W. Norton & Co.

Kets de Vries, M. F. R. (1980). *Organizational paradoxes: clinical approaches to management.* London and New York: Tavistock Publications.

Kinder, A. (2007). Counselling psychologists in the workplace. *Counselling Psychology Review, 22*(1), 32–34.

Kinderman, P. (2005). The applied psychology revolution. *The Psychologist, 18*(12), 744–746.

Kirschenbaum, H., & Henderson, V. L. (Eds.) (1990). *The Carl Rogers reader.* London: Constable.

Kirschner, S. R. (1996). *The religious and romantic origins of psychoanalysis: individuation and integration in post-Freudian theory.* Cambridge: Cambridge University Press.

Kuhn, T. S. (1970). *The structure of scientific revolutions* (2nd Ed.). Chicago and London: University of Chicago Press.

Lacan, J. (1968). *The language of the self: the function of language in psychoanalysis.* (A. Wilden, trans.). Baltimore, MD: John Hopkins University Press.

Lacan, J. (1977). *Écrits: a selection.* London: Tavistock/Routledge.

Lalande, V. M. (2004). Counselling psychology: a Canadian perspective. *Counselling Psychology Quarterly, 17*(3), 273–286.

Lambert, M. J., & Barley, D. E. (2002). Research summary on the therapeutic relationship and psychotherapy outcome. In J. C. Norcross (Ed.), *Psychotherapy relationships that work: therapist contributions and responsiveness to patients.* Oxford: Oxford University Press.

Lambert, M. J., Bergin, A. E., & Garfield, S. L. (2004). Introduction and historical overview. In M. J. Lambert (Ed.), *Bergin and Garfield's handbook of psychotherapy and behavior change* (5th Ed.). New York: John Wiley & sons, Inc.

Lambert, M. J., & Ogles, B. M. (2004). The efficacy and effectiveness of psychotherapy. In M. J. Lambert (Ed.), *Bergin and Garfield's handbook of psychotherapy and behavior change* (5th Ed.). New York: John Wiley & sons, Inc.

Landman, J. T., & Dawes, R. M. (1982). Smith and Glass' conclusions stand up under scrutiny. *American Psychologist, 37*, 504–516.

Lane, C., Wilkinson, F., Littek, W., Heisig, U., Browne, J., Burchell, B., Mankelow, R., Potton, M., & Tutschner, R. (2004). *The future of professionalised work in Britain and Germany: counselling psychologists and psychotherapists.* London: Anglo-German Foundation for the Study of Industrial Society.

Lane, D. A., & Corrie, S. (2006a). Counselling psychology: its influences and future, *Counselling Psychology Review, 21*(1), 12–24.

Lane, D. A., & Corrie, S. (2006b). *The modern scientist-practitioner: a guide to practice in psychology.* London and New York: Routledge.

Laungani, P. (2004). Some unresolved issues in philosophy and psychology: their implications for therapy. *Counselling Psychology Quarterly, 17*(1), 107–123.

Lather, P. (1992). Postmodernism and the human sciences. In S. Kvale (Ed.), *Psychology and postmodernism.* London: Sage.

Lawton, B., & Feltham, C. (Eds.) (2000). *Taking supervision forward: enquiries and trends in counselling and psychotherapy.* London: Sage.

Layard, R. (2004). Mental health: Britain's biggest social problem? Paper to the Strategy unit in the Cabinet Office, www.cabinetoffice.gov.uk

Layard, R., Bell, S., Clark, D., Knapp, M., Baroness Meacher, Priebe, S., Thornicroft, G., Lord Turnberg, & Wright, B. (2007). *The depression report.* London: HMSO.

Lazarus, A. A. (1971). *Behavior therapy and beyond.* New York: McGraw-Hill.

Lazarus, A. A. (1976). *Multimodal behavior therapy.* New York: Springer Publishing Company.

Leach, M. M., Akhurst, J., & Basson, C. (2003). Counseling psychology in South Africa: current political and professional challenges and future promises. *The Counseling Psychologist, 31*(5), 619–640.

Leahey, T. H. (2004). *A history of psychology: main currents in psychological thought.* London: Pearson Prentice Hall.

Lee, J. C. (1996). A study of counsellor education and training. *Korean Journal of Counseling and Psychotherapy, 8*, 1–26.

Legg, C., & Donati, M. (2006). Getting the most out of personal therapy. In R. Bor, & M. Watts (Eds.), *The trainee handbook: a guide for counselling and psychotherapy trainees* (2nd Ed.). London: Sage.

Lenihan, P., & Iliffe, S. (2000). Counselling the community: the contribution of counselling psychologists to the development of primary care. *Counselling Psychology Quarterly, 13*(4), 329–343.

Leong, F. T. L., & Leach, M. M. (2007). Internationalizing counseling psychology in the United States: a SWOT analysis. *Applied Psychology: An International Review, 56*(1), 165–181.

Leong, F. T. L., & Savickas, M. L. (2007). Introduction to special issue on international perspectives on counseling psychology. *Applied Psychology: An International Review, 56*(1), 1–6.

Leung, S. A., Chan, C. C., & Leahy, T. (2007). Counseling psychology in Hong Kong: a germinating discipline. *Applied Psychology: An International Review, 56*(1), 51–68.

Linehan, M. M. (1993). *Cognitive-behavioral treatment of borderline personality disorder.* New York: The Guilford Press.

Løvlie, L. (1992). Postmodernism and subjectivity. In S. Kvale (Ed.), *Psychology and postmodernism.* London: Sage.

Luborsky, L., Singer, B., & Luborsky, L. (1975). Comparative studies of psychotherapies: is it true that 'Everyone has won and all must have prizes'? *Archives of General Psychiatry, 32*, 995–1008.

Luborsky, L., McClellan, A. T., Woody, G. E., O'Brien, C. P., & Auerbach, A. (1985). Therapist success and its determinants. *Archives of General Psychiatry, 42*, 602–611.

Lyotard, J-F. (1984). *The postmodern condition: a report on knowledge.* (G. Bennimgton & B. Massumi, trans). Minneapolis, MN: University of Minneapolis Press. (Original work published in 1979.)

Mander, G. (2004). The selection of candidates for training in psychotherapy and counselling. *Psychodynamic Practice, 10*(2), 161–172.

Mair, M. (1999). Inquiry in conversation – questions, quests, search and research. *Psychotherapy Section Newsletter, 25*, 2–15 (British Psychological Society).

Maroda, K. J. (1998). *Seduction, surrender, and transformation: emotional engagement in the analytic process.* Hillsdale, NJ: The Analytic Press.

McAlister, L. L. (1976). *The philosophy of Brentano.* London: Duckworth.

McCann, D. (2006). Supervision: making it work for you. In R. Bor & M. Watts (Eds.), *The trainee handbook: a guide for counselling and psychotherapy trainees.* (2nd Ed.). London: Sage.

McLeod, J. (1994). *Doing counselling research.* London: Sage.

McLeod, J. (1999). *Practitioner research in counselling.* London: Sage.

McLeod, J. (2001). *Qualitative research in counselling and psychotherapy.* London: Sage.

Merleau-Ponty, M. (1962). *Phenomenology of perception.* (C. Smith, trans.). London: Routlege & Kegan Paul.

Mills, J. (2005). A critique of relational psychoanalysis. *Psychoanalytic Psychology, 22*(2), 155–188.

Minsky, R. (1996). *Psychoanalysis and gender: an introductory reader.* New York: Routledge.

Mitchell, S. A. (2000). *Relationality: from attachment to intersubjectivity.* Hillsdale, NJ: The Analytic Press.

Mitchell, S. A., & Aron, L. (Eds.) (1999). *Relational psychoanalysis: the emergence of a tradition.* Hillsdale, NJ: The Analytic Press.

Moran, J. (1999). Response to John Rowan's article: 'a personal view: concerns about research'. *Counselling Psychology Review, 14(*1), 45–46.

Moya, P. M. L., & Hames-Garcia, M. R. (Eds.) (2000). *Reclaiming identity: realist theory and the predicament of postmodernism.* Berkeley, CA: University of California Press.

Munley, P. H., Duncan, L. E., McDonnell, K. A., & Sauer, E. M. (2004). Counseling psychology in the United States of America. *Counselling Psychology Quarterly, 17*(3), 247–271.

Murdock, N. L., Alcorn, J., Heesacker, M., & Stoltenberg, C. (1998). Model training program in counseling psychology. *The Counseling Psychologist, 26*, 658–672.

Nelson-Jones, R. (1999). On becoming counselling psychology in the Society: establishing the counselling psychology Section, *Counselling Psychology Review, 14*(3), 30–37.

Newnes, C. (2007a). The implausibility of researching and regulating psychotherapy. *Journal of Critical Psychology, Counselling and Psychotherapy, 7*(4), 221–228.

Newnes, C. (2007b). Are we all mad? *Journal of Critical Psychology, Counselling and Psychotherapy, 7*(3), 191–194.

Norcross, J. C., Beutler, L. E., & Levant, R. F. (Eds.) (2006). *Evidence-based practices in mental health: debate and dialogue on the fundamental questions.* Washington, DC: American Psychological Association.

O'Brien, M., & Houston, G. (2007). *Integrative therapy: a practitioner's guide* (2nd Ed.). London: Sage.

O'Gorman (2001). The scientist-practitioner model and its critics. *Australian Psychologist, 36*, 164–169.

Ogden, T. (1992). *Projective identification and psychotherapeutic technique*. London: Karnac.

Orlans, V., & Edwards, D. (2001a). A collaborative model of supervision. In M. Carroll & M. Tholstrup (Eds.), *Integrative approaches to supervision*. London: Jessica Kingsley Publishers.

Orlans, V., & Edwards, D. (2001b). Counselling the organisation, *Counselling at Work* (Journal of the Counselling at Work Division of the British Association for Counselling and Psychotherapy), (33), 5–7.

Orlans, V. (2003). Counselling psychology in the workplace. In R. Woolfe, W. Dryden & S. Strawbridge (Eds.), *Handbook of counselling psychology*. London: Sage.

Orlans, V. (2007). From structure to process: ethical demands of the postmodern era. *The British Journal of Psychotherapy Integration, 4*(1), 54–61.

Orlans, V. (2008). Coaching and counselling in organisations: an integrative multi-level approach. In A. Kinder, R. Hughes & C. Cooper (Eds.), *Employee well-being: a workplace resource*. Chichester: Wiley.

Oxford English Dictionary (Concise) (2006). Eleventh edition edited by Catherine Soanes & Angus Stevenson. Oxford: Oxford University Press.

Parker, I. (Ed.) (1999). *Deconstructing psychotherapy*. London: Sage.

Parker, I., Georgaca, E., Harper, D., McLaughlin, T., & Stowell-Smith, M. (1995). *Deconstructing psychopathology*. London: Sage.

Patton, W. (2005). Coming of age? Overview of career guidance policy and practice in Australia. *International Journal for Educational and Vocational Guidance, 5*(2), 217–227.

Pavlov, I. P. (1932). Reply of a physiologist to psychologists. *Psychological Review, 39*, 91–127.

Pelling, N. (2000) Scientist versus practitioners: a growing dichotomy in need of integration. *Counselling Psychology Review, 15*(4), 3–7.

Pentonen, M. (Ed.) (1996). *The Cambridge companion to Bacon*. Cambridge: Cambridge University Press.

Penney, J. F. (1981). The development of counselling psychology in Australia. *Australian Psychologist, 16*(1), 20–29.

Perls, F., Hefferline, R., & Goodman, P. (1951/1994). *Gestalt therapy: excitement and growth in the human personality*. Highland, NY: The Gestalt Journal Press.

Peters, R. (1956). *Hobbes*. Harmondsworth: Penguin.

Pilgrim, D. (1997). *Psychotherapy and society*. London: Sage.

Pilgrim, D. (2005). Registration, regulation and public protection. *Journal of Critical Psychology, Counselling and Psychotherapy, 5*(4), 169–175.

Polanyi, M. (1967). *The tacit dimension*. London: Routledge & Kegan Paul Ltd.

Pryor, R. G. L., & Bright, E. H. (2007). The current state and future direction of counseling psychology in Australia. *Applied Psychology: An International Review, 56*(1), 7–19.

Psychological Society of Ireland (2001). Division of Counselling Psychology (DCoP) Rules. Dublin: Psychological Society of Ireland.

Reason, P., & Bradbury, H. (2008). *The Sage handbook of action research: participative inquiry and practice*. (2nd Ed.). London: Sage.

Rennie, D. L. (1994). Human science and counselling psychology: closing the gap between research and practice. *Counselling Psychology Quarterly, 7*(3), 235–250.

Rizq, R. (2005). Ripley's game: projective identification, emotional engagement, and the counselling psychologist. *Psychology and Psychotherapy: Theory, Research and Practice, 78*, 449–464.

Rizq, R. (2006). Training and disillusion in counselling psychology: a psychoanalytic perspective. *Psychology and Psychotherapy: Theory, Research and Practice, 79*, 613–627.

Robitschek, C., & Woodson, S. J. (2006). Vocational psychology: using one of counselling psychology's strengths to foster human strength. *The Counseling Psychologist, 34*(2), 260–275.

Robson, C. (2002). *Real world research.* Malden, MA: Blackwell Publishing.

Rogers, C. R. (1951). *Client-centered therapy: its current practice, implications, and theory.* Boston, MA: Houghton Mifflin.

Rogers, C. R. (1961). *On becoming a person: a therapist's view of psychotherapy.* London: Constable.

Rosenzweig, S. (1936). Some implicit common factors in diverse methods of psychotherapy. *American Journal of Orthopsychiatry, 6*, 412–415.

Roth, A., & Fonagy, P. (2005). *What works for whom? A critical review of psychotherapy research* (2nd Ed.). New York: The Guilford Press.

Rowan, J. (2005). *The transpersonal: spirituality in psychotherapy and counselling* (2nd Ed.). London and New York: Routledge.

Russell, B. (1961). *History of western philosophy* (2nd Ed.). London: George Allen & Unwin Ltd.

Ryle, A., & Kerr, I. B. (2002). *Introducing Cognitive Analytic Therapy: Principles and Practice.* Chichester: John Wiley and Sons.

Safran, J. D., & Muran, J. C. (2000). *Negotiating the therapeutic alliance: a relational treatment guide.* New York: The Guilford Press.

Sampson, E. E. (1998). Life as an embodied art: the second stage – beyond constructionism. In B. M. Bayer & Shotter, J. (Eds.), *Reconstructing the psychological subject: bodies, practices and technologies.* London: Sage.

Sandler, J. (Ed.) (1989). *Projection, identification, projective identification.* London: Karnac.

Sandler, J., Dare, C., & Holder, A. (1992). *The patient and the analyst* (2nd Ed.). London: Karnac.

Sartre, J. P. (1965). *Essays in existentialism.* Secaucus, NJ: The Citadel Press.

Schön, D. A. (1983). *The reflective practitioner: how professionals think in action.* London: Temple Smith.

Schore, A. N. (1994). *Affect regulation and the origin of the self: the neurobiology of emotional development.* Hillsdale, NJ: Lawrence Erlbaum Associates.

Schore, A. N. (2003a). *Affect dysregulation and disorders of the self.* New York: W. W. Norton & Company.

Schore, A. N. (2003b). *Affect regulation and the repair of the self.* New York: W. W. Norton & Company.

Segal, Z. V., Williams, J. M. J., & Teasdale, J. D. (2002). *Mindfulness-based cognitive therapy for depression: a new approach to preventing relapse.* New York: The Guilford Press.

Seligman, M. (1995). The effectiveness of psychotherapy: the consumer reports study. *American Psychologist, 50*(12), 965–974.

Seligman, M. E. P. (2002). *Authentic happiness.* New York: Free Press.

Seligman, M. E. P., Steen, T. A., Park, N., & Peterson, C. (2005). Positive psychology progress: empirical validation of interventions. *American Psychologist, 60*(5), 410–421.

Seo, Y. S., Kim, D. M., & Kim, D. (2007). Current status and prospects of Korean counseling psychology: research, clinical training, and job placement. *Applied Psychology: An International Review, 56*(1), 107–118.

Sequeira, H. (2005). Editorial: 'We are very good at listening but we have to start speaking!' *Counselling Psychology Review, 20*(3), 1.

Shotter, J. (1992). 'Getting in touch': the meta-methodology of a postmodern science of mental life. In S. Kvale (Ed.), *Psychology and postmodernism*. London: Sage.

Siegel, D. J. (1999). *The developing mind: toward a neurobiology of interpersonal experience*. New York: The Guilford Press.

Simos, G. (Ed.) (2002). *Cognitive behaviour therapy: a guide for practising clinicians*. Hove and New York: Brunner-Routledge.

Skinner, B. F. (1957). *Verbal behavior*. New York: Appleton-Century-Crofts.

Smail, D. (2007). The cultural context of therapy. *Journal of Critical Psychology, Counselling and Psychotherapy, 7*(3), 131–145.

Smallwood, J. A. (2002). Counselling psychology and the NHS: an individual perspective. *Counselling Psychology Review, 17*(91), 16–20.

Smith, M. L., & Glass, G. V. (1977). Meta-analysis of psychotherapy outcome studies. *American Psychologist, 32*, 752–760.

Smith, M. L. Glass, G. V., & Miller, T. I. (1980). *The benefits of psychotherapy*. Baltimore, MD: John Hopkins University Press.

Spinelli, E. (1994). *Demystifying therapy*. London: Constable.

Spinelli, E. (2001a). *The mirror and the hammer: challenges to therapeutic orthodoxy*. London: Sage.

Spinelli, E. (2001b). Counselling psychology: A hesitant hybrid or a tantalizing innovation? *Counselling Psychology Review, 16*(3), 3–12.

Spinelli, E. (2005). *The interpreted world: an introduction to phenomenological psychology* (2nd Ed.). London: Sage.

Spinelli, E. (2007). *Practising existential psychotherapy: the relational world*. London: Sage.

Stanley, P., & Manthei, R. (2004). Counselling psychology in New Zealand: the quest for identity and recognition. *Counselling Psychology Quarterly, 17*(3), 301–315.

Staples, J. L. (2007). Reflections of a counselling psychologist in private practice. *Counselling Psychology Review, 22*(1), 35–40.

Stein, D. M., & Lambert, M. J. (1995). Graduate training in psychotherapy: are therapy outcomes enhanced? *Journal of Consulting and Clinical Psychology, 63*, 182–196.

Stern, D. N. (2003). *The interpersonal world of the infant: a view from psychoanalysis and developmental psychology* (2nd Ed.). London: Karnac.

Stern, D. N., & The Boston Change Process Study Group (2003). On the other side of the moon: the import of implicit knowledge for gestalt therapy. In M. Spagnuolo Lobb & N. Amendt-Lyon (Eds.), *Creative license: the art of gestalt therapy*. Vienna: Springer-Verlag.

Stolorow, R. D., Atwood, G. E., & Ross, J. (1978). The representational world in psychoanalytic therapy. *International Review of Psychoanalysis, 5*, 247–256.

Stolorow, R. D., & Atwood, G. E. (1992). *Contexts of being: the intersubjective foundations of psychological life*. Hillsdale, NJ: The Analytic Press.

Strawbridge, S., & Woolfe, R. (2003). Counselling psychology in context. In R. Woolfe, W. Dryden & S. Strawbridge (Eds.), *Handbook of counselling psychology* (2nd Ed.). London: Sage.

Stricker, G. (2002). What is a scientist-practitioner anyway? *Journal of Clinical Psychology, 58*, 1277–1283.

Stricker, G., & Trierweiler, S. (2006). The local clinical scientist: a bridge between science and practice. *Training and Education in Professional Psychology, S*, 37–46.

Sugg, M. (2007). A week in the life of an NHS counselling psychologist. *Counselling Psychology Review, 22*(1), 19–21.

Taylor, C. (1989). *Sources of the self: the making of the modern identity*. Cambridge, MA: Harvard University Press.

Tehrani, N. (1995). An integrated response to trauma in three Post Office businesses. *Work and Stress, 9*(4), 380–393.

Tehrani, N. (1997). Internal counselling provision for organisations. In M. Carroll & M. Walton (Eds.), *Handbook of counselling in organizations.* London: Sage.

The International Association of Applied Psychology (IAAP): The Division of Counseling Psychology (Division 16). http://www.iaapcounselingpsychology.org

The Law Society (2006). *Family law protocol* (2nd Ed.). London: the Law Society.

Thompson, J. (1974). *Kierkegaard.* London: Gollancz.

Totton, N. (1997). The Independent Practitioners Network: A new model of accountability. In R. House & N. Totton (Eds.), *Implausible professions: arguments for pluralism and autonomy in psychotherapy and counselling.* Ross-on Wye: PCCS Books.

Tourette-Turgis, C. (1996). *Le counseling.* Paris: Presses Universitaires de France.

Tourette-Turgis, C. (1997). *Guide du counseling.* Neuilly sur Seine: Roche.

Towl, G., & Crighton, D. (2002). Risk assessment and management. In G. Towl, L. Snow & M. McHugh (Eds.), *Suicide in prisons.* Oxford: BPS Blackwell.

Van Deurzen-Smith, E. (1988). *Existential counselling in practice.* London: Sage.

Van Scoyoc, S. (2004). The personal (psychologist) is political. *Counselling Psychology Review, 19*(3), 42–44.

Van Scoyoc, S. (2004). Counselling psychology and psychological testing: professional issues. *Counselling Psychology Review, 19*(4), 6–8.

Vespia, K. M., & Sauer, M. S. (2006). Defining characteristic or unrealistic ideal: historical and contemporary perspectives on scientist-practitioner training in counselling psychology. *Counselling Psychology Quarterly, 19*(3), 229–251.

Walsh, Y. (2007). My role as a consultant counselling psychologist within the NHS. *Counselling Psychology Review, 22*(1), 22–26.

Wampold, B. E. (2001). *The great psychotherapy debate: models, methods and findings.* Mahwah, NJ: Lawrence Erlbaum Associates.

Wampold, B. E., Mondin, G. W., Moody, M., Stich, F., Benson, K., & Ahn, H. (1997). A meta-analysis of outcome studies comparing bona fide psychotherapies: Empirically 'All must have prizes'. *Psychological Bulletin, 122,* 203–215.

Watanabe-Muraoka, A. M. (2007). A perspective on counseling psychology in Japan: towards a lifespan approach. *Applied Psychology: An International Review, 56*(1), 97–106.

Watanabe-Muraoka, M. (1996). *Kaunseringu shinnrigaku: kaunsera to hena surushakai* (translation: *Counseling psychology: the counsellor and changing society*) (1st Ed.). Kyoto: Nakanishiya Publishers.

Watson, M., & Fouche, P. (2007). Transforming a past into a future: counseling psychology in South Africa. *Applied Psychology: An International Review, 56*(1), 152–164.

Whiteley, J. N. (1984). Counseling psychology: a historical perspective. *The Counseling Psychologist, 12,* 3–109.

Wilber, K. (2006). *Integral spirituality.* Boston and London: Integral Books.

Williams, C. (1978). The dilemma of counselling psychology. *Australian Psychologist, 13,* 33–40.

Williams, D. I., & Irving, J. A. (1996). Personal growth: Rogerian paradoxes. *British Journal of Guidance and Counselling, 24*(2), 165–172.

Wolf, D. B. (1998). The Vedic Personality Inventory: a study of gunas. *Journal of Indian Psychology, 16*(1), 10–17.

Woldt, A. L., & Toman, S. N. (Eds.) (2005). *Gestalt therapy: history, theory, and practice.* Thousand Oaks, CA: Sage.

Wolpe, J., & Lazarus, A. A. (1966). *Behaviour therapy techniques: a guide to the treatment of neuroses.* Oxford: Pergamon Press.

Woolfe, R. (1996). The nature of counselling psychology. In R. Woolfe & W. Dryden (Eds.), *Handbook of counselling psychology.* London: Sage.

Woolfe, R. (2002). Freud, psychology and psychotherapy. *Counselling Psychology Review, 17*(4), 45.

Woolfe, R. (2006). A journey from infancy to adulthood: the story of counselling psychology. *Counselling Psychology Review, 21*(91), 2–3.

Wright, L., Borrill, J., Teers, R., & Cassidy, T. (2006). The mental health consequences of dealing with self-inflicted death in custody, *Counselling Psychology Quarterly, 19*(2), 165–180.

Yalom, I. D. (1980). *Existential psychotherapy.* New York: Basic Books Inc.

Young, J. E. (1999). *Cognitive therapy for personality disorders: a schema-focussed approach* (3rd Ed.). Sarasota, FL: Professional Resource Press.

Young, J. E., Klosko, J. S., & Weishaar, M. E. (2003). *Schema therapy: a practitioner's guide.* New York: The Guilford Press.

Young, R. A., & Nicol, J. J. (2007). Counselling psychology in Canada: advancing psychology for all. *Applied Psychology: An International Review, 56*(1), 20–32.

Zhang, N., Li, J., & Yuan, Y. G. (2001). Investigation of counselling in China. *Journal of Health Psychology, 9,* 389–391.

INDEX

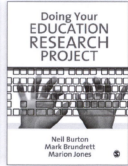
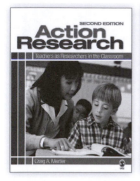

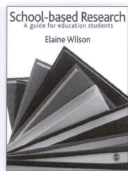

Research Methods Books
from SAGE

Basics of
QUALITATIVE
RESEARCH
3e

Juliet Corbin
Anselm Strauss

The
Mixed
Methods
Reader

Vicki L. Plano Clark ▪ John W. Creswell

DOING
QUALITATIVE
RESEARCH
USING
YOUR COMPUTER

A PRACTICAL GUIDE

CHRIS HAHN

SECOND EDITION
INTERVIEWS
Learning the Craft of Qualitative Research Interviewing

Steinar Kvale
Svend Brinkmann

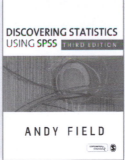

DISCOVERING STATISTICS
USING SPSS THIRD EDITION

ANDY FIELD

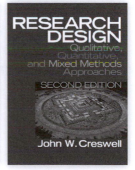

RESEARCH
DESIGN
Qualitative,
Quantitative,
and Mixed Methods
Approaches
SECOND EDITION

John W. Creswell

www.sagepub.co.uk

SAGE

Supporting researchers for more than forty years

Research methods have always been at the core of SAGE's publishing. Sara Miller McCune founded SAGE in 1965 and soon after, she published SAGE's first methods book, Public Policy Evaluation. A few years later, she launched the Quantitative Applications in the Social Sciences series – affectionately known as the "little green books".

Always at the forefront of developing and supporting new approaches in methods, SAGE published early groundbreaking texts and journals in the fields of qualitative methods and evaluation.

Today, more than forty years and two million little green books later, SAGE continues to push the boundaries with a growing list of more than 1,200 research methods books, journals, and reference works across the social, behavioral, and health sciences.

From qualitative, quantitative, mixed methods to evaluation, SAGE is the essential resource for academics and practitioners looking for the latest methods by leading scholars.

www.sagepublications.com